I0441061

THE COMING FALL OF NORTH KOREA

NUKES WILL END
THE KIM DYNASTY

Young Sop Ahn

Copyright © 2019 Young Sop Ahn
All rights reserved.
Printed in the United States of America
First edition, 2019
ISBN: 9781071013946

CONTENTS

INTRODUCTION

Numerous people are living in countries that are ruled by despots today. We wonder why so many people have to obey just a few evil dictators and why so many people have to die from hunger due to the wicked rule of a few. We also wonder why the world does not have a single international law enforcement agency with the powers to prosecute them for crimes against humanity. We continue to wonder why this global community of responsible states does not or cannot rise up against such tyrants to change our world for the better. Furthermore, we are utterly bewildered to see Donald Trump, the president of the world's strongest country and one of the most advanced democracies on the earth, shake hands with Kim Jong-un, one of the most brutal despots in the world, on an equal basis, with the display of a row of American and North Korean flags side by side at their meeting sites.

The Borgen Project places Kim Jong-un at the top of the list of "Eight Current Dictators as of 2018," and says "Kim Jong-un is North Korea's current dictator and the third generation Kim to rule the country."[1] We are witnessing this regime of North Korea spend so much money on nuclear weapons development when the same money could have been used to rescue so many North Koreans from starving to death.

Living in the most peaceful time in the history of humanity, we know nuclear weapons have no military value. Still, we are afraid of nukes in the hands of dangerous tyrants like Kim Jong-un, as such regimes may sell them to terrorists. We hope that the international community will be able to stop the nuclear development program of the most dangerous regime on the planet. At the same time, we are deeply interested in the widespread view that the Kim Jong-un regime will fall in the near future.

When it comes to North Korean affairs, "the collapse of North Korea" has been one of the most common topics analysts have addressed. My book is just another one of this kind. However, I would first like to clarify the difference between my book and others in this regard. My book title, *The Coming Fall of North Korea*, indicates that the breakdown of the Kim Jong-un regime in the North is imminent, but not necessarily leading to North Korea's breakdown as a country. I argue that the downfall of the Kim Jong-un regime is unlikely to lead to a termination of North Korea as a state, drawing parallels to the manner in which West Germany absorbed East Germany, thus reunifying Germany in 1990. I also attempt to foretell that the Kim dynasty of the North will reach its demise in five years and suggest the reasons why.

However, I try to propose how and under what conditions the Kim regime would be able to survive the challenges this unusual age presents to the virtually bankrupt but abnormally armed regime that has continued to pose a grave threat to world peace with no justifiable reasons. Not only myself but also many other analysts wish the North Korean regime could survive through profound transformation of its economy and regime character to become a responsible member of the global community rather than desire it to face a tragic end. This thought may remind us of a work by John Donne, who highlighted that all people are connected to and dependent on other people. A quotation from an English metaphysical poet of the seventeenth century says:

> No man is an island entire of itself; every man is a piece of the continent, a part of the main; if a clod be washed away by the sea, Europe is the less, as well as if a promontory were, as well as any manner of thy friends or of thine own were; any man's death diminishes me, because I am involved in mankind. And,

therefore, never send to know for whom the bell tolls; it tolls for thee.[2]

To predict why and when the North Korean regime will collapse has always been a challenging task for any analyst, especially as a "scientific" effort. The prediction I make in this nonfiction is literally not fictitious and is a result of scientific research. To put it another way, my argument in this book is based on hard facts. Even so, it is conceded that nonfictitious, scientific analyses are often beaten by fictitious imagination, insight, and intuition. For example, English writer H. G. Wells, who is called the father of science fiction, wrote a lot of stories that all turned on the possible developments in the future of some contemporary force or group of forces, many of which have turned out to be true. In his book, *The World Set Free*, written in 1913 and published in early 1914, Wells wrote:

> the atomic bombs were thrown at the dykes. They made a mighty thunder in the air . . . leaving a flaring trail in the sky. The night . . . seemed to vanish, to be replaced abruptly by a black background to these tremendous pillars of fire . . . Few who adventured into these areas of destruction and survived attempted any repetition of their experiences. There are stories of puffs of luminous, radio-active vapor drifting sometimes scores of miles from the bomb center and killing and scorching all they overtook.[3]

Wells not only described the aftermath of the explosion as "radio-active vapor" but also precisely portrayed how harmful and long-lasting its effects would be. On the other hand, as if looking down upon Wells' imagination, Robert A. Millikan, American experimental physicist, honored with the Nobel Prize in 1923, observed in 1928:

> There is no likelihood man can ever tap the power of the atom. The glib supposition of utilizing atomic

> energy when our coal has run out is a completely
> unscientific Utopian dream, a childish bug-a-boo.[4]

What happened after the renowned physicist had made the prediction?
The Manhattan Project—which was a research and development project
that produced the first nuclear weapons during the Second World War—
began modestly in 1939, that is, only eleven years after Millikan made the
infamous observation. The United States dropped the first atomic bombs
on the Japanese cities of Hiroshima and Nagasaki in August 1945, which
killed at least 129,000 people. This thus became a historic event in which
a fictional conception turned out to be right while a prediction made by
a celebrated scientist proved wrong. It is admitted that Wells—who was
nominated for the Nobel Prize in Literature four times but never won
one—was not only a visionary novelist but also something of a great scientist,[5] but his vision teaches us that we should always be aware of scientific flaws.

As for the fate of North Korea, many analysts have made wrong predictions but, apparently, they have not been ashamed of their incorrect
predictions possibly because of the unpredictable nature and behavior of
the North Korean regime that has defied anybody's reasoning and common sense. The series of wrong predictions about the destiny of North
Korea have provided even the impression that any analyst of North
Korean affairs could offer a prediction based only on plausible ideas that
cannot be scientifically validated. US security expert Jamie Metzl seems
to try to point out the fundamental problems that pundits specializing in
volatile North Korean issues, including himself, typically face. He wrote
in 2017, perhaps taking yet another risk of making a wrong prediction:

> As a member of the U.S. National Security Council
> staff in the later 1990s, I worked with colleagues on
> plans for responding to the potential collapse of the
> North Korean government. Almost twenty years
> later, the Democratic People's Republic of Korea is
> still there and those predicting its imminent collapse

have continually been proven wrong. But today, the
North Korean madness may well be nearing its end-
game. I predict it will be gone within a decade.[6]

Metzl's or any other analyst's prediction of the North's future cannot go
through any scientific experiment. Naturally, few could know anything
about the scientific basis of Metzl other than the points he made in the
article referred to above. This does not necessarily indicate that his fore-
cast can be subject to criticism. It has been said in the academia that questions in social science have no correct or definite answers. As far as the
problem of accuracy with my prediction of the North Korean fate is concerned, perhaps suffice it to say that just one nonpolitical factor that I'm
looking at in this book—relentless advances in science and technology—
may be enough to certainly end the North's three-generation dictatorship
that depends on nuclear weapons to threaten the world and its own people
for its anomalous survival. I will highlight this factor later in this book as
it amounts to a "scientific" possibility. In addition to this "new" factor,
I'm going to suggest what I consider as objective factors that will contrib-
ute to ending the Kim dynasty regime.

To put all of my ideas together, the key points of my argument in this
book are as follows. First, the Kim Jong-un regime will die from nothing
other than its own nukes in five years. With no exception, the prospect for
a North Korean downfall has been raised in connection with its pursuit of
nuclear weapons instead of economic reforms. The Kim dynasty's nuclear
development will boomerang on it. Second, the Kim regime, nonetheless,
will find it very hard, if not totally impossible, to abandon nuclear weapons. Third, China and other factors, including advances in science and
technology, will precipitate the Kim regime collapse. Last but not least,
the Kim regime has only one option for survival: it has to be authentic
and audacious in dismantling its nuclear program as a precondition for
winning international support for its stability.

The subject matter of my book, the impending fall of the Kim Jong-un
regime, necessarily involves tackling the regime's obsession with nuclear
development in particular and its actual doings up to the present. In other

words, to predict the fate of the Kim regime inevitably requires an in-depth analysis of the regime character of the state called "an abnormal country,"[7] from its formation to the proposed upcoming downfall, from a historical perspective. In this context, I cannot emphasize enough the fact that throughout human history the regime character, like that of the North Korean regime, has never been able to avoid a tragic end, with no exception.

In more detail, the book attempts to describe how the state called North Korea came to be established at the beginning with what regime character and how the regime character has since evolved with what specific goals and policies. Given this feature, my book may be considered as one that is not so much entirely about an impending downfall of the Kim dynasty as about North Korea overall and its nuclear weapons development in particular. However, the focus of my book is absolutely on its collapse from start to finish, implicitly and explicitly.

As I argue that the Kim dynasty of the North will fall due to its own fallacy of morbid devotion to nuclear weapons development, the bulk of this book is devoted to the characteristics of North Korea's nuclear weapons program, the process of its development, and how this "anachronistic" weaponry is about to strangle none other than its lover, the North Korean regime. In short, my book is about the impact of the Kim dynasty's nuclear weapons program on its own life.

Needless to say, different analysts can craft different notions about how long the Kim dynasty regime will be able to last. However, nobody could make any prediction about the longevity of anything in question without touching on the key factors that are most closely related to it. I am no exception to this rule. This book pays utmost attention to the dangerous nature of the North Korean regime, which has made nuclear weapons development the first priority of all national policies that I argue will prove self-destructive at the end of the day. I expect readers to provide me with as much feedback as possible to my analysis from an evidence-based historical perspective of the unique character of North

Korea's Kim dynasty regime so gripped with nuclear weapons development and its fate.

Young Sop Ahn

Notes:

1 "Eight Current Dictators as of 2018," Borgen Project (2018), https://borgenproject.org/, accessed March 31, 2018.

2 J. Donne, *Devotions upon Emergent Occasions, and Several Steps in My Sickness* (1624). The *Devotions* were written in December 1623.

3 See, for example, Delphi Classics, *Delphi Complete Works of H. G. Wells* (Hastings, UK: Delphi Publishing, 2015).

4 Quoted in AZ Quotes (2018), https://www.azquotes.com/, accessed October 20, 2018.

5 See, for example, A. J. Spera, "H. G. Wells Predicts a Utopian Future: Is He Right?" Bookstr (2016), https://www.bookstr.com/, accessed September 20, 2016.

6 J. Metzl, "Why North Korea Is Destined to Collapse," *National Interest* (2017), https://nationalinterest.org/, accessed September 18, 2017.

7 Numerous analysts and organizations have dealt with the abnormality of North Korea. As for North Korea's anomaly, see, for example, B. Haas and D. Hurst, "Beatings, Killings, Gulags: North Korea Rights Abuses Likely to Be Ignored at Summit," *Guardian* (2018), https://www.theguardian.com/, accessed June 6, 2018.

CHAPTER 1

THE FORMATION OF A "BIG LIE" STATE

I t requires no scientific validation that even the best liars get caught in the end. Likewise, a "lie" state will destroy itself and fall. Scarcely had Japan been defeated in the Second World War (1939–1945) and had its colonial rule in Korea ended in 1945 when the Korean Peninsula was divided into two zones along the 38th parallel. The former Soviet Union, officially the Union of Soviet Socialist Republics (USSR), seized the northern half of the peninsula and the United States occupied the southern half. Consequently, many analysts have thought that the USSR and the United States are responsible for the division of the peninsula. However, in a long-range historical perspective, neither the USSR nor the United States is the root cause of the split of the Korean nation. Adolf Hitler should first be held responsible for the Korean disunion since the major causes of the Second World War were Hitler's takeover of absolute power in Germany beginning in 1933 and his Nazi Party that had pursued an aggressive foreign policy that led to the war.[1] The tragic end of treacherous Hitler and his hostile foreign policy have important implications for the future of the bellicose Kim dynasty of North Korea, since the Kim dynasty is very likely to face the same disastrous finale that Hitler suffered.

The division meant a creation of two states that are worlds apart on the Korean Peninsula—a paradise, the South, and a hell, the North. South Korea is an advanced democracy and dynamic market economy today, with per capita gross domestic product (GDP) of 41,388 US dollars,[2] while North Korea is one of the most oppressive, poorest countries on the planet with a command economy, per capita GDP standing at 1,800 US dollars, merely 4 percent of the South's.[3] This huge discrepancy between the two Koreas is greatly due to the radical difference in ideology between the two occupiers of the Korean Peninsula—the USSR and the United States—that have become two models that the North and the South have followed. The former's official state ideology was Marxism-Leninism, which was doomed to grand failure, whereas democracy and capitalism have been central to American identity. As it has turned out in reality, the democratic United States remains the single superpower in the world, while the USSR, referred to as an "evil empire"[4] of "communism, the dark tyranny that controlled nearly forty nations and was responsible for the deaths of an estimated 100 million victims during the twentieth century, suddenly collapsed without a single bullet being fired."[5]

North Korea was created as a "Big Lie" state.[6] In a celebration of Korea's liberation from Japan, held on October 14, 1945 at the center of Pyongyang, a Russian general on the podium was going to introduce a new leader of the North who he called comrade Kim Il-sung. The crowd of some 100,000 people were excited as they were about to see the legendary guerilla leader Kim who had fought for Korean independence against the Japanese army over twenty years in Korea and Manchuria. The swell of excitement running through the crowd, however, soon turned into a wave of mistrust and displeasure as a young man in his thirties stepped up to the podium. They were anxious to see the heroic independence fighter Kim Il-sung, who would be in his late fifties, with grayish hair and wrinkles on the face. Kim Il-sung had been known to be fighting for years mostly in mountainous areas of northeastern China. The young Kim Il-sung on the podium was fake. Brazilian lyricist and novelist Paulo Coelho, best known for his novel *The Alchemist*, notes, "No one can lie, no one can hide anything, when he looks directly into someone's eyes." It is unclear whether the audience looked directly into the young Kim's eyes on the podium. If the audience had, Kim must have been an exceptional liar capable of changing even the light in his eyes that matches well his title, founder of a "Big Lie" state.

A feature of *South China Morning Post* (*SCMP*) described in 2010 how the fake Kim had come to control North Korea and when the information about his relationship with Russia began to be transmitted to the world. The *SCMP* article can be considered a piece of the most interesting information that shows how the identity of the North Korean dictator Kim Il-sung was forged:

> This is the extraordinary story of how Josef Stalin picked an obscure officer in the Red Army to be the ruler of the new country his army had occupied and grafted onto him the life of its most famous guerilla leader, to give him an authority and credibility he did not possess. This story only came to light after the fall of the Soviet Union in 1991, when the Russians involved in establishing the new state of North Korea could speak to foreign scholars and journalists.[7]

What had happened to the real Kim Il-sung? Who is the fake Kim Il-sung? Understandably, historical records of the tumultuous Second World War period of Korea under the Japanese occupation are often controversial, and they are especially scanty and incorrect when it comes to an account of a person like the alleged counterfeit Kim. Even so, there has been substantial consensus on the history of the real Kim and the phony Kim, which witnesses from the period have agreed with.[8]

The real Kim who had used the name, "Kim Il-sung," was a prominent early leader of the Korean resistance against the Japanese and was referred to as General Kim by Koreans in Manchuria. Kim is the most common surname in Korea, accounting for nearly 22 percent of the population. The real Kim was born in 1888 in Korea's northernmost province of Hamgyeong-do in a rich family of the ruling class (called *yangban* in Korean). His original name was Kim Eung-cheon and he changed his name to Kim Kyung-cheon, and later to Kim Il-sung. As he died in 1942, he could never appear in downtown Pyongyang in 1945. A lot of reliable studies have noted that the earlier years of Kim Il-sung, who later came to rule North Korea, are shrouded in obscurity.[9] "In totalitarian states, history is something that can be changed to suit the needs of the ruling party."[10] Various reliable sources describe Kim Kyung-cheon to the following effect:[11]

> Kim Kyung-cheon later entered the Imperial Japanese Army Academy and graduated in 1911. In June 1919 he fled to Manchuria to join the Korean independence movement but after only six months he moved to Vladivostok to fight under Kim Kyu, who was renowned for victory over a Japanese battalion. His main operation after arriving in Vladivostok was fighting off Japanese-supported Chinese militias. In this period, he chose Kim Kyung-cheon as a pseudonym.[12]

Kim Kyung-cheon
(Source: Public domain in the United States, photographed before January 1, 1947)

During the Russian Civil War, his troops managed to impress Red Army commanders with good discipline. However, during the Great Purge, a campaign of political repression in the Soviet Union that occurred from 1936 to 1938, Kim was arrested for protesting the Korean Dislocation policy of the supreme leader of the Soviet Union, Joseph Stalin, and eventually died in a Soviet prison in 1942.[13] Reliable sources believe the "fake" younger Kim Il-sung stole Kim Kyung-cheon's identity after his death.[14] Lee Myung-young, a renowned South Korean scholar of North Korean affairs, published a book, *The Legend of Kim Il-sung*,[15] in 1974, in which he asserted that the original "General" Kim Il-sung was an Imperial Japanese Army Academy graduate. The "fake" Kim Il-sung, original name Kim Song-ju, was born on April 15, 1912, near Pyongyang to a family that was not very poor but was always a step away from poverty. Kim Song-ju was not an intellectual and not well read. He was reported to have known a lot of Confucianism and a smattering of Marx, Lenin, and Hegel.[16] According to some sources, Kim became a member of the Korean guerrilla fight against the Japanese colonialists in Manchuria. *Encyclopaedia Britannica* writes:

> Kim (Song-ju) was the son of parents who fled to Manchuria during his childhood to escape the Japanese rule of Korea. He attended elementary school in Manchuria and, while still a student, joined a communist youth organization. He was arrested and jailed for his activities with the group in 1929–30. After Kim's release from prison, he joined the Korean guerrilla resistance against the Japanese occupation sometime during the 1930s and adopted the name of an earlier legendary Korean guerrilla fighter against the Japanese.[17]

Encyclopaedia Britannica continues to write, "Kim was noticed by the Soviet military authorities, who sent him to the Soviet Union for military and political training. There he joined the local Communist Party."[18] Judging based on available sources combined, the two Kims have at least four aspects in common. First, neither of the two was born Kim Il-Sung. Even the younger Kim Il-sung admitted to having been born Kim Song-ju.[19] Second, they participated in anti-Japanese campaign, albeit with different roles and feats. The younger Kim's role in the fight against Japan was trivial.[20] Third, both had contacts with the Soviet Union. Fourth, both were jailed outside the Korean Peninsula, albeit for different reasons and periods. The younger Kim was imprisoned only for several months. This commonality can at least in part be responsible for the stolen identity of Kim Il-sung. The *SCMP* article further explains on the "fake" Kim based on the sources from the Korean Provisional Government-in-exile, which was based in Shanghai, China:

> Kim Il-sung played a very minor role in the war with Japan, spending the last four-and-a-half years in a Soviet army base near Khabarovsk, returning to Korea not at the head of a victorious army or even with the Red Army but on a Soviet naval vessel that carried him and other Koreans from Vladivostok to Wonsan a month after Japan's surrender.[21]

"No one welcomed them at the pier of Wonsan. They went for a dinner of beer and noodles at a local restaurant. In terms of personal sacrifice and their actions in fighting Japan, many had a greater claim to a leadership role than the young Kim Il-sung."[22] The view that Kim Song-ju thieved the identity of the real, heroic Kim Il-sung can further be supported by the fact that Kim has been the focus of a personality cult that has dominated domestic politics since the founding of North Korea. In other words, the ambitious Kim probably felt the need to steal the identity of the legendary resistance fighter to deify himself even before he founded a communist state in the North.

Despite all the reliable evidences that back up the younger Kim's false identity, the issue of whether Kim Il-sung is fake or real is certainly overshadowed by the spine-chilling developments that have happened since the rule of Kim Il-sung started in North Korea. Even if we admit Kim

Il-sung's identity remains controversial, the dismal facts about North Korea that have been recorded since its founding demonstrate that the Kim Il-sung regime was formed as a "Big Lie" and as an apparatus for tyranny, strongly supporting the view that the young Kim who appeared in Pyongyang in 1945 was "fake" Kim Il-sung.

Kim Il-sung (the "fake" Kim is referred to as "Kim Il-sung" hereafter) was a wizard who could change history into something to best suit the needs to realize his ambition. As it turned out soon, even Stalin could not have imagined that the man who he bestowed a country on would create an imperial dynasty that has lasted more than seventy years and fabricate a history that would amaze his own hagiographers.[23]

Kim had other strengths that greatly helped him get his master's authorization to establish a totalitarian state in the North. He came back to Korea after twenty-five years in exile. He spoke Russian fluently and had received his formal education in Chinese. So, he received intensive training from his Soviet masters to improve his written and spoken Korean, to enable him to read speeches and address meetings. "The speech he gave at the Pyongyang rally that October 14 was written by his Soviet mentors and translated into Korean."[24] Kim's background in language education played an important part in his early access to power. The *SCMP* feature adds:

> When the Red Army invaded Manchuria on August 8, 1945, Stalin was expecting a long and bitter war with fanatical Japanese. To his surprise, there was little resistance and his army entered Pyongyang in mid-August. He needed someone to head a puppet regime and asked Lavrentiy Beria, the head of the NKVD (the People's Commissariat for Internal Affairs of the Soviet Union) secret police. Beria had interviewed Kim Il-sung several times and recommended him. Stalin met him and gave him the job.[25]

All told, the USSR shaped Kim Il-sung.[26] In December 1945, the Soviets installed Kim as chairman of the North Korean branch of the Korean

Communist Party.[27] The Communist Party was nominally led by Kim Tu-bong, although from the outset Kim Il-sung held the real power.[28] A communist state under Kim Il-sung's absolute rule was thus brought into being in the northern zone. The elections that were held in North Korea on August 25, 1948, to select delegates to the "Supreme People's Council" were phony. They were not free, and fit the "Big Lie" state. The voters were presented, for their approval or disapproval only, with lists of candidates drawn up by the "North Korean People's Committee," and the balloting was not secret. The elections had proved that whether Kim Il-sung's identity was forged or not, Kim was an outrageous impostor who could do anything bad against anybody, including his own people, and any country to satisfy his objectives and greed. The newly elected Supreme People's Council in North Korea proclaimed, on September 9, 1948, the establishment of a bogus state officially called "Democratic People's Republic of Korea (DPRK)" under Kim Il-sung's rule, claiming jurisdiction over the entire country, including the South.[29] On October 12, 1948, the Soviet Union recognized Kim's government as the sovereign government of the entire peninsula. The Communist Party of the North merged with the New People's Party of Korea to form the Workers' Party of North Korea.[30]

Kim Il-sung, center, at the joint meeting of the New People's Party and the Communist Party of Korea on August 28, 1946. Portraits of Stalin and Kim are seen. (Source: Public domain in the United States, photographed on August 28, 1946)

Kim Il-sung created a "Big Lie" worthy of Stalin and Hitler after all. He lied to his people about the past and the present, blaming famine, rationing, and shortages on South Korea, officially called the Republic of Korea (ROK), Japan, and the United States. However, Kim Il-sung is very different from even Stalin and Hitler in terms of the "Big Lie." Stalin and Hitler were denounced after their deaths, as were the communist leaders of Eastern Europe, who created similar personality cults.[31] Theoretically, Kim Il-sung is still in control even after death as "Eternal President of North Korea." As a result, the North Korean regime is often referred to as "government by ghost." The *Washington Post* reported in in June 1995 when North Korea approached the first anniversary of the death of Kim Il- sung:

They call it "government by ghost." Many observers of that unpredictable nation report an eerie sensation that, in some sense, the dead ruler is still in charge. "The newspapers are full of pronouncements and decrees saying, 'This is what Kim Il Sung wanted us to do.' They still show Kim Il Sung speeches all the time on the state TV stations—and that's the only TV anybody up there can see."[32]

The *Washington Post*'s article continues: "The evocation of the late leader is not restricted to domestic affairs. Intelligence officials in Seoul say that when North Korea's new ambassador to Phnom Penh presented his formal credentials last month (May 1995) to the king of Cambodia, the documents were issued in the name of 'President Kim Il Sung'—who died on July 8, 1994."[33] The worship of Kim Il-sung is by far the most widespread among the people. Every North Korean adult still wears a Kim Il-sung lapel pin every day, just like they did when the late Kim was in charge.[34] He created numerous titles for personality cult, including a heaven-sent leader, the father of the Korean nation, and the eternal Sun of mankind. Some analysts have argued such "Big Lie" is one of the major reasons why the North Korean regime has been unable to open its closed country to the international community, an issue to be further discussed later in this book. All told, the big liar Kim Il-sung sowed an evil seed of tragedy on the Korean Peninsula.

Notes:

1 See, for example, "Adolf Hitler," *History* (2019), https://www.history.com/, accessed February 8, 2019.

2 "South Korea," *World Economic Outlook Database*, International Monetary Fund (2018), https://www.imf.org/, accessed April 30, 2018.

3 "GDP—Per Capita (PPP)," *World Factbook* (US Central Intelligence Agency, 2014), https://www.cia.gov/, accessed on April 30, 2018.

4 US president Ronald Reagan called the Soviet Union an "evil empire" during a speech to the National Association of Evangelicals in March of 1983.

5 L. Edwards, "Ronald Reagan and the Fall of Communism," Heritage Foundation (2010), https://www.heritage.org/, accessed January 27, 2010.

6 About the obscurity of Kim Il-sung's young days, see, for example, M. O'Neill, "Kim Il-sung's Secret History," *South China Morning Post* (2010), https://www.scmp.com/, accessed October 17, 2010.

7 Ibid.

8 For this consensus, see, for example, J. Becker, *Rogue Regime: Kim Jong Il and the Looming Threat of North Korea.* (New York: Oxford University Press, 2005).

9 "Kim Il-sung," GlobalSecurity.Org (2018), https://www.globalsecurity.org/, accessed July 10, 2018.

10 M. O'Neill, "Kim Il-sung's Secret History," *South China Morning Post* (2010).

11 See, for instance, "Kim Il-sung," GlobalSecurity.Org (2018). Similar descriptions are found in various websites.

12 Quite a few Japanese and Korean scholars and analysts provide such information about Kim Kyung-cheon. See, for example, Lee Myung-young, *The Four Kim Il-sungs* (Tokyo: Seonggapseobang, 2000) (written in Japanese). The South Korean late professor Lee published a number of books and articles (written

in Korean and Japanese) about "fake" Kim Il-sung. About Kim Kyung-cheon, refer to "Anti-Japanese Hero Kim Kyung-cheon," *Kyunghyang Shinmun* (2005) (written in Korean), http://news.khan.co.kr/, accessed September 5, 2005.

13 Ibid.

14 Ibid.

15 Quoted in J. Becker, *Rogue Regime: Kim Jong Il and the Looming Threat of North Korea* (2005).

16 "Kim Il-sung," GlobalSecurity.org (2014), https://www.globalsecurity.org/org/, accessed June 25, 2017.

17 The Editors of *Encyclopaedia Britannica*, "Kim Il-Sung," *Encyclopaedia Britannica* (2018), https://www.britannica.com/, accessed July 17, 2018.

18 Ibid.

19 "Are All Stories about North Korea True?" *Gwangju News* (2015), https://gwangjunewsgic.com/, accessed January 27, 2015.

20 Quite a few analysts of North Korean affairs argue that Kim Il-sung had never participated in any anti-Japanese struggle for Korean independence. They contend that Kim's career in this respect was totally fabricated. See, for instance, "Knowing Kim-Il Sung Correctly," North Korea Strategy Center United States (2017), http://nksc.us, accessed May 1, 2019.

21 M. O'Neill, "Kim Il-sung's Secret History," *South China Morning Post* (2010).

22 Ibid.

23 Ibid.

24 Ibid.

25 Ibid.

26 N. Shevchenko, "How North Korea's Kim Il Sung Was Shaped by the USSR," Russia Beyond (2019), https://www.rbth.com/, accessed January 14, 2019.

27 B. Martin, *Under the Loving Care of the Fatherly Leader: North Korea and the Kim Dynasty* (New York: Thomas Dunne Books, 2004).

28 See, for instance, "North Korean Purges: Kim Il-sung," GlobalSecurity.org (2018), https://www.globalsecurity.org/, accessed October 20, 2018.

29 US Department of State, *A Historical Summary of United States–Korean Relations with a Chronology of Important Developments 1834–1962*, a US Department of State publication, no. 7446, Far Eastern Series 115 (Washington, DC: Bureau of Public Affairs, Historical Office, November 1962).

30 "Workers' Parties of Korea Merge," Wayback Machine (2008), https://web. archive.org/, March 5, 2008.

31 M. O'Neill, "Kim Il-sung's Secret History," *South China Morning Post* (2010).

32 See, for example, T. Reid, "The Ghost That Haunts Asia's Hermit Kingdom," *Washington Post* (1995), https://www.washingtonpost.com/, accessed June 21, 1995. The *Post* report quoted Kil Jeong Woo of South Korea's Research Institute for National Reunification as saying, "If you ask me who rules the roost in Pyongyang, I'd say that the regime is trying to make it look as if the ghost of the late Kim is still in control."

33 Ibid.

34 Ibid.

CHAPTER 2

KIM IL-SUNG'S GOAL TO BRING THE KOREAN PENINSULA UNDER HIS CONTROL

History shows that militant states with evil intentions can rise for a certain period but eventually they fall. North Korea will be no exception to this iron rule of history. As soon as Kim Il-sung took the reins of government in the North, he planned to turn the entire Korean Peninsula into a communist country. In less than two years after Kim brought the northern zone under his dictatorship, his plan was manifested in the Korean War that broke out on June 25, 1950. A few dissenters have made an unsubstantiated argument that North Korea made a raid on the South as a response to the South's assault. The fact is that Kim Il-sung decided to invade the South to reunite two Koreas under his communist control.[1]

Kim Il-sung was tricky but impatient and reckless. American lifestyle writer Dan Scotti opines that being impatient and overly ambitious may occasionally produce positive results especially while young.[2] However, most pundits agree that haste and carelessness is harmful to anybody, any undertaking, and any country. DaShanne Stokes, a respected American thinker, warns, "If you love your country, you must be willing to defend it from fraud, bigotry, and recklessness."[3] The geopolitical circumstances surrounding the Korean Peninsula in 1950, when Kim was in his late thirties, did not favor Kim's extreme aspiration to seize South Korea by force. Kim was cunning enough to know that the military power of North Korea alone could not subjugate South Korea. He needed preparation for the war.

His first task for the war preparation was to meet with his hero, Stalin. On March 5, 1949, only six months after he took power in the North, Kim Il-sung and his top subordinates, including the deputy prime minister and foreign minister of North Korea, Pak Hon-young, met Stalin in Moscow. *The International History Declassified* of the Wilson Center Digital Archive details the conversation of the first meeting between Stalin and Kim Il-sung:

> Stalin asks the members of the delegation how their trip was, was it difficult on the journey?
> Kim Il Sung thanks the Soviet Government for its attention to them and says that they arrived safely.
> Stalin asks how they traveled—by railroad or by air.
> Kim Il Sung answers that they came by railroad.
> Stalin asks whether they became ill on the way.
> Kim Il Sung answers that they were healthy.[4]

During the conversation with Stalin, Kim did not disclose outright his intention to invade the South. Instead, Kim asked Stalin to provide a wide range of aid to North Korea—ranging from military to economic and educational assistance. For example, the North Korean leader asked permission to send Korean officers to the Military Academy of the USSR for training, and Stalin responded that such permission was possible. When Stalin asked if Kim had thought about USSR credit or a loan, Kim answered that he wanted to receive credit. Stalin indicated that he could give credit in the sum of 40 million US dollars. Noteworthy was that Kim Il-sung tried to explain military conditions of South Korea to get military aid from the USSR, and Stalin expressed a great interest in the military strength of the South. Their conversation about the military issue proceeded as follows:

> Kim says that in the south of Korea there are still American troops and that intrigues against North

Korea by the reactionaries are increasing, that they have infantry troops, but sea defense almost does not exist. The help of the Soviet Union is needed in this.

Stalin asks how many American troops are in South Korea.

Kim answers that there are up to 20,000 men.

Stalin asks if there is a national Korean army in the south.

Kim answers that there is, the number is around 60,000 men.

Stalin asks if this number includes only regular army or also police.

Kim answers that it includes only regular army.

Stalin (joking) asks, and you are afraid of them?

Kim—No, we are not afraid, but we would like to have naval units.

Stalin asks which army is stronger—north or south.

Pak Hon-young answers that the northern army is stronger.[5]

From left: Kim Il-sung, A. I. Mikoyan, Andrei Gromyko and Pak Hon-young passing before the guard of honor at the Yaroslav Station, Moscow, in March 1949. (Source: The Archives of Korean History)

The Stalin-Kim meeting revealed that Stalin wanted to know the details of military situations on the Korean Peninsula, including South Korea's military strength and US military presence in the South. Stalin's questions below reflect his desire to better understand whose military is stronger, the North's or the South's. They indicate that Stalin intensely wanted the North Korean military to outdo the South's. This must have pleased Kim Il-sung.

> Stalin asks if there are dry docks in (North) Korea left by the Japanese.
>
> Kim answers that there are none.
>
> Stalin says that it is possible to render assistance in this, and that (North) Korea needs to have military planes.
>
> Stalin asks if they (North Koreans) are penetrating the South Korean army, if they have their own people there?
>
> Pak Hon-young answers that they are penetrating, but so far, they are not revealing themselves there.[6]

Stalin's response to Pak's answer and his questions as follows indirectly unveiled his intention to support Kim Il-sung's ambition to attack South Korea to unify the Korean Peninsula under his communist rule when the Soviet leader came to feel it appropriate for Kim to provoke a war against the South. The Stalin-Kim conversation reflected their concern about the comparative military strengths of the North and the South.

> Stalin says that this is correct, that it is not necessary to reveal themselves now and indicates that the southerners also, apparently, are sending their people into the army of the North and that they need to exercise caution.
>
> Stalin asks what has happened along the 38th parallel. "Is it true that several points have fallen to

the southerners and have been seized, and then these points were taken back?"

Kim answers that they are taking into account that the southerners can send their own people into the North Korean army, and that they are taking the necessary measures. Kim reported that there was a clash with the southerners in Gangwon province at the 38th parallel. Their police were not sufficiently armed at that time. When regular units approached, the southerners retreated.[7]

The Stalin-Kim conversation that continued was more specific and intriguing. Given the fact that Kim invaded the South only about a year after this meeting, it is certain that the key objective of Kim Il-sung's visit to the USSR was to explore Stalin's attitude toward the South to expedite Kim's plan to outpower the South in military strength.

Stalin asks, "Did they drive away the southerners or did they leave themselves?"

Kim answers that as a result of the battle they drove away the southerners, threw them across the border of the country.

Stalin asks if they have a military school.

Kim answers that they do.

Stalin asks if there is a pilot school.

Terentii Shtykov (the first supreme leader of North Korea during the Soviet occupation of the North 1945–1948) reports that they have a training-military aviation regiment.

Kim says that they have a military school, but no military academy and that among the officer corps of the Korean army there is no one who has completed a military academy. He asks permission to send Korean officers to the Military Academy of the USSR for training.

> Stalin asks wasn't there such permission.
> Kim answers that there was not.
> Stalin says that it is possible to permit it.[8]

Kim Il-sung and Stalin met again in April or May (the exact date has yet to come to light) 1950, and discussed the North Korean economy and Soviet-North Korean cooperation. Prior to this meeting, there was a series of communications between them. Kim's key objective of those communications was to invade the South. In the 1950 meeting, Kim said to Stalin that five years had passed since Korea's liberation from Japan by the Soviet Army. Kim Il-sung invaded the South only a month or so after this meeting. The following cable indicates that Kim offered Stalin his plan to attack the South in the meeting. On May 30, 1950, in a strictly secret cable to the USSR politburo, Shtykov reported on Kim Il-sung's military planning for an invasion of South Korea and signaled Soviet approval for the invasion. The cable read:

> I met with Kim Il Sung, at his request, on 29 May. At the beginning of the conversation, Kim Il Sung reported that the weapons and ammunition, which he had requested during his stay in Moscow, had mainly already arrived. The weapons had been transported to the newly formed divisions, and the delivery of weapons to the soldiers would be completed by 1 June. Kim Il Sung reported that, at his order, the chief of the general staff had finished the drafting of a decision in principle for an attack.[9]

Kim Il-sung, who had succeeded in establishing a fake regime in the North as a USSR puppet state, eventually started a real war known as the Korean War. Kim had persistently sought Stalin's approval and help for his plan to invade the South, but Stalin, a cautious and shrewd political master, snubbed Kim's idea. Although Kim was a mannequin of Stalin, Kim's ambition to occupy the South even tried to challenge Stalin's disapproval.

Stalin had every reason to discourage Kim's adventure to attack South Korea. Among others, it was imperative that Stalin develop a strategy for East Asia that lessened the risk of conflict between the Soviet Union and the United States. Stalin feared that Kim's provocation might escalate into a world war between the West and the Communist bloc. He rejected Kim's request by claiming that the DPRK should not take the offensive; it could fight back and take over South Korea if South Korea took the offensive first.[10] Stalin, however, realized that Kim's drive to place the Korean Peninsula under his control could not be suppressed indefinitely.[11]

On top of that, Mao Zedong, the leader of the Chinese Communist Party (CCP), was a critical factor. Although the Soviet and Chinese camps shared the common ground of communist ideology, disagreement between the two leaders was developing rapidly after the Second World War. In 1949, the rift between Stalin and Mao had deepened. During the war, Mao Zedong fought against Imperial Japan. Simultaneously, he was fighting in the Chinese Civil War (1927–1949) against the Nationalist Kuomintang led by Generalissimo Chiang Kai-shek. During the Second World War, Stalin advised Mao to enter an anti-Japanese coalition with Chiang Kai-shek, which Mao ignored. After the war, Stalin advised Mao against seizing power and to collaborate with the Nationalists because of Stalin's Treaty of Friendship and Alliance (1945) with the Kuomintang, which Mao turned a blind eye to. Especially, the lack of Stalin's support of the CCP during the civil war that Mao had won continued to bother Mao.[12] All told, Mao rebuffed most of Stalin's advice. Meanwhile, in the 1945–1949 period, Chiang Kai-shek received large amounts of financial and military assistance from the United States,[13] which had irked Stalin. Stalin was also concerned that Mao too might continue to seek diplomatic relations with the United States in the future to hold Chiang in check.[14]

Although Kim Il-sung was disappointed when Stalin initially rebuffed his plan to attack South Korea, his ambition knew no bounds. The sneaky Kim could not miss the bad blood that was developing between Stalin and Mao. Kim needed Mao's support as well as Stalin's to realize his objective. The imprudent Kim failed to realize how toxic his drive to put the Korean Peninsula under the control of communism would prove to the future of the "Big Lie" state and the Kim dynasty. For now, Kim needed to ensure at least China's aid in case Stalin continued to refuse his plan.

The uncomfortable relationship between Stalin and Mao contributed in part to setting the stage for Mao-Kim meeting in May 1950 in Beijing. Upon his return from Moscow, the frustrated Kim tried to meet Mao. Kim soon received a letter from North Korean ambassador to China, Ri Ju-yeon. Ri said in the letter that he had a meeting with Chinese leader Mao Zedong and Foreign Minister Zhou Enlai, during which the question of the necessity of a meeting between Kim Il-sung and Mao Zedong was discussed. Ri's letter read:

> Mao, turning toward Ri as if asking when you intend to begin the unification of the country, without waiting for an answer stated that if you intend to begin military operations against the South soon, then they should not meet officially. In such a case the trip should be unofficial. Mao Zedong added further that the unification of Korea by peaceful means is not possible, solely military means are required to unify Korea. About the Americans, there is no need to be afraid of them. The Americans will not enter a third world war for such a small territory.[15]

Mao, on his part, had every reason to meet Kim Il-sung. Mao was sensitive to how Stalin-Kim connection was evolving concerning Kim's plan to invade the South:

> In January 1950, Mao had approved the North Korean leader's initial request to visit Beijing. Mao wanted to discuss Kim's possible war plans. North Korean Ambassador to China Ri Ju-yeon claimed that he would indeed relay the message to Kim who was "undergoing medical treatment." Kim's medical treatment was a cover story for all those not informed

of his trip to meet with Stalin. In another attempt to gain information from the ambassador, Mao voiced his concerns over North Korean military preparations. When Ri was again aloof in answering, Mao grew more concerned that Kim may indeed be working plans behind his back with Stalin.[16]

Mao's interest in Kim Il-sung's plan to invade the South was one thing and his assessment on Kim's scheme was another. As for Kim's desire to unify Korea, Mao, like Stalin, was concerned about a conflict with the United States in the event of a war on the Korean Peninsula. His statement to Ri that "the Americans will not enter a third world war"[17] concealed his true judgment. Also, China could not afford to support Kim Il-sung's war against South Korea, since in early 1950 the People's Republic of China (PRC) was only a few months old, and the Mao regime faced daunting internal tasks of regime consolidation, unifying its own land, broadening people's support, and economic reconstruction.[18] Mao was aware that the CCP regime was still in the course of unification and it would be too difficult for the CCP forces to wage wars on two fronts.[19] Earlier in 1949, Mao promised Kim that once the CCP united China, it would assist Kim in uniting the two Koreas too. Mao made the promise since during the Chinese Civil War, Mao's troops often withdrew to North Korea to escape from the Kuomintang troops' attacks, and the Korean divisions played important roles in Chinese duels with the Kuomintang counterparts in Manchuria.[20]

Even so, given the fact that the CCP forces that had yet to be united and near-certain US intervention in a war on the Korean Peninsula, Mao was unable to approve Kim's desire to conquer the South. Nevertheless, Mao was indisposed to reject Kim openly, so he sent a telegram to Stalin asking for help. On November 5, 1949, Stalin replied with a telegram, asserting that he agreed with Mao, and he would persuade Kim not to take the offensive, which would surely result in Western allies' intervention in the war.

Despite the initial denial in 1949, Stalin finally decided in 1950 to support Kim Il-sung's request for military operations against South Korea.[21]

However, it was neither Stalin-Mao disagreement nor Kim Il-sung's ultimate success in persuading either Stalin or Mao or both that contributed to Kim's invasion of the South. The turning point came in early 1950. A major development caused Stalin to change his previous stance. US secretary of state Dean Acheson delivered a speech on January 12, 1950, in which he declared that the US defensive perimeter ran through Japan, the Ryukyus, and the Philippines and not South Korea or the Republic of China (commonly referred to as Taiwan). This official statement made Stalin believe that the United States might not intervene in a Korean War.[22] Thus, the Korean War was to break out soon.

Hundreds of thousands of South Koreans fled the South in mid-1950 after the North Korean army invaded. (Source: Public domain from the US Defense Department)

Notes:

1 "Kim Il-sung Sends His Troops South," Macrohistory and World Timeline (2015), http://www.fsmitha.com/, accessed January 20, 2015.

2 D. Scotti, "Young and Reckless: How Everything Society Says Is Wrong with You Will Make You Successful," *Elite Daily* (2014), https://www.elitedaily.com/, accessed January 17, 2014.

3 A quote in "Reckless Quotes," Goodreads, https://www.goodreads.com/, accessed June 30, 2013.

4 "Meeting between Stalin and Kim Il Sung" (March 5, 1949), Wilson Center Digital Archive (various years), http://digitalarchive.wilsoncenter.org/, accessed December 11, 2015.

5 Ibid.

6 Ibid.

7 Ibid.

8 Ibid.

9 "Record of a Conversation of Cde. (Comrade) Stalin with Kim Il Sung and Pak Heon-yeong (May 1950)," Wilson Center Digital Archive.

10 "Why China Entered the Korean War," *Medium* (2017), https://medium.com/, accessed March 1, 2017.

11 See, for instance, B. Monger, "Stalin's Decision: The Origins of the Korean War," Calhoun: The National Postgraduate School Institutional Archive (2014), 72.

12 Ibid., 25.

13 E. Dreyer, *China at War 1901–1949* (New York: Routledge, 1995).

14 B. Monger, "Stalin's Decision: The Origins of the Korean War," 14.

15 "Telegram from Shtykov to Vyshinski Regarding Meeting with Kim Il Sung (May 12, 1950)," Wilson Center Digital Archive.

16 B. Monger, "Stalin's Decision: The Origins of the Korean War," 64.

17 "Telegram from Shtykov to Vyshinski Regarding Meeting with Kim Il Sung."

18 See, for example, M. Sheng, "Mao's Role in the Korean Conflict: A Revision" (2014), *The Official Journal of the Historical Society for Twentieth-Century China*, Vol. 39, Issue 3.

19 "Why China Entered the Korean War," *Medium* (2017).

20 Ibid.

21 B. Monger, "Stalin's Decision: The Origins of the Korean War," 64.

22 "Why China Entered the Korean War," *Medium* (2017).

CHAPTER 3

THE KOREAN WAR IS NOT A FORGOTTEN WAR BUT A KIM IL-SUNG WAR

I f it had not been for the Korean War, inter-Korean relations could have played out constructively rather than in an adversarial fashion as they are today. The term "North Korea's collapse," would not been used as often as it is today in the topics that the analysts of North Korean affairs address.

The Korean War was destructive not only to the Korean Peninsula but also to the rest of the world. Kim's bestial provocation against the South caused the United Nations (UN) forces led by the US military to intervene in the war. Different sources provide different estimates of casualty figures. According to Korean War Educator, a total of 449,312 UN troops from sixteen countries, including 416,004 from South Korea and 29,550 from the United States, were dead. The wounded and missing from the UN side totaled 545,473 soldiers. On the communist side, over 1,520,000 soldiers were dead, wounded, or missing, of which more than one million killed were Chinese soldiers.[1] Besides, millions of civilians lost their lives on both sides.[2]

The Korean War has been called "the Forgotten War" in the United States primarily because it has never captured the American public's imagination quite like the Second World War or Vietnam War, and remains one of the least discussed and least understood conflicts in US history despite a great number of American casualties and extensive international

Korean civilians fleeing from the North Korean forces, killed when caught in the line of fire during night attack by guerrilla forces near Yongsan, Seoul, on August 25, 1950. (Source: Public domain photograph from Defense Imagery Management Operations Center)

involvement.[3] However, the title, the Korean War, can be misleading for many South Koreans as well as other people in the world: it could have been more appropriately dubbed "the Kim Il-sung War" since without Kim Il-sung, the war would never have happened. Kim Il-sung had sowed the evil seed that grew into the bloody Korean War and the brutality of the North Korean regime against peace-loving countries, which should be the last thing the whole world, especially the United States as well as South Korea, could ever "forget."

It is true that the three-year conflict on the Korean Peninsula pitted communist and capitalist forces against each other. However, UN forces exercised legitimate power for self-defense in defense of freedom and market economy against a surprise attack by a rogue regime headed by communist and despot Kim Il-sung. In other words, a deeper insight into the war says it is wrong to consider the war simply as a confrontation between communism and capitalism like a duel between two gunmen, each with his own reason to fight, as we often see in a Western movie. The Korean War cannot be eligible to be "the Forgotten War" especially for the following two reasons:

First, the war has yet to formally end, although North Korean leader Kim Jung-un wants it to end, a major reason for which has been offered by Jung H. Pak, a Brookings' analyst of East Asian affairs:

> Kim seeks to maintain the initiative on shaping the global debate about how to approach the North Korea problem. That is, he is looking to shift the discussion to non-nuclear issues to deflect attention away from its nuclear weapons and dampen the international community's appetite for implementing sanctions.[4]

Second, "the Kim Il-sung War" cannot be forgotten since Kim Il-sung remains "Eternal President of North Korea," dead or alive. Kim Il-sung and his dynastic successors have continued brutal attempts to realize the "eternal" dream to occupy the whole Korean Peninsula even after South and North Korea reached an armistice in 1953 to stop the world from thinking about an end of the war. The war is still going on in the form of hot or cold war, as demonstrated in North Korea's violent provocations against the South and the United States as well as in the North's ongoing nuclear weapons program.

A group of North Korean commandos, dubbed Unit 124, sneaked into South Korea in 1968 to kill South Korean president Park Chung-hee. They had been sent by Kim Il-sung. Four woodcutter brothers came across the infiltrators from Pyongyang in a hill in Paju, just 10 miles from South Korea's border with the North:

> The suspicious eldest brother asked Kim Shin-jo, leader of the assassins, "Gentlemen, are you from the North?"
>
> "Yes, comrades. We are here to liberate you and bring communism to South Korea," Kim told the woodcutters.

Kim was going to kill the woodcutters. But the ground was frozen, making it impossible to bury the bodies. So, Kim drew up a contract, lecturing the brothers on the virtues of communism and promising them a place in the revolutionary government that would be formed once Unit 124's mission was complete.

"You can join us, or you can die," Captain Kim told them.

The woodcutters signed the pact and were released. The North Korean commandos Kim led had been trained for two years for the mission: to assassinate President Park Chung-hee.[5]

The thirty-one–person commando team headed by Kim Shin-jo made a raid on the Blue House (South Korean equivalent to the White House) on January 21, 1968, to eliminate President Park, but failed to fulfill their mission. Only two survived the failed attempt, including Kim, who was captured by South Korean forces, and the other made it back to the North. He was interrogated for a year by the South Korean authorities before being released, and became a citizen of South Korea in 1970. Kim later became a pastor at the Sungrak Sambong Church in Gyeonggi-do, South Korea, and is now residing there with his wife and two children.[6]

In the 1960s and 1970s alone, there were eight major North Korean provocations against South Korea and the United States. In January 1968, North Koreans captured the US Navy ship the USS Pueblo and its crew in East Sea in North Korean waters. The attack had killed one sailor and held eighty-three other crew members until December 23. In October 1968, a wave of more than 100 North Korean commandos landed on the northeast shore of South Korea to wage a guerrilla war against the South Korean government, in which a total of one hundred ten commandos and twenty South Koreans were killed. In April of the following year, a US reconnaissance plane was shot down off the North Korean coast, killing thirty-one Americans. Cold-blooded provocations by North Koreans ensued in the 1970s as follows:

In June 1970, North Korean patrol boats seized a South Korean broadcast vessel with twenty crew on board.

In February 1974, North Korea sank two South Korean fishing boats.

In August 1976, North Korean troops axed two US officers cutting down a tree in the Demilitarized Zone (DMZ).[7] The US Central Intelligence Agency (CIA) considered the brutality was preplanned by the North Korean government. The incident, known as the Korean axe murder incident, drew international attention to the cruel nature of the Kim Il-sung regime.[8]

When the barbarian incident, also known as the Panmunjom axe murder incident, happened, South Korean president, Park Chung-hee, got furious. "A mad dog should receive lashes with a heavy club," he said.[9] No other remark could better characterize how to deal with the North Korean regime.

It could be meaningless to read just a time line of the philistine acts of North Korea against South Korea, the United States, Japan, and the rest of international society without a closer look at them, as the cruelty of the North Korean dynasty regime has only intensified and become well known worldwide. The key point we should not miss here is that the series of North Korean provocations have continued not simply as hate crimes but with a malicious intent to put in danger the security and peace of South Korea and international society at large. Kim Il-sung regime's provocations exactly reflect the regime character of the Kim dynasty. Kim Il-sung's heartless provocations had continued in the 1980s and 1990s until his death.

In October 1983, North Korea orchestrated a mammoth-scale provocation against South Korea even outside the country. It attempted to assassinate South Korean president Chun Doo-hwan who was on an official visit to capital of Burma (present-day Myanmar). President Chun survived a deadly North Korean bomb attack in Rangoon (present-day Yangon), but 21 people, including four South Korean cabinet members, were killed and 46 others were wounded.[10]

In November 1984, nine North Korean soldiers and one South Korean soldier were killed in firefight after a Soviet man tried to escape into South Korea.

In May 1992, three Northern soldiers in South Korean uniforms were killed in Cheolwon city, Gangwon-do province, in South Korea.[11]

Did Kim Il-sung's death in 1994 make any difference in terms of North Korean provocations? One of the most dominant features of Kim Il-sung's legacy was nuclear weapons development. This characteristic has been enhanced by his successors. Kim Il-sung, unlike Deng Xiaoping of China, wrongly taught his descendants, his son and grandson, how to make the North powerful to survive the inauspicious times, mainly by depending upon nuclear weapons development and maintaining brutality against humanity.

Kim Il-sung died in less than five years after the demise of the Soviet Union and European communism. The collapse of the Soviet Empire and communism in Eastern Europe, and the decease of Kim Il-sung combined seemed to be precipitating a downfall of the North's Kim regime. Many analysts argued that the communist regime in the North was approaching fast the end of its life. For instance, the late US congressional representative and political thinker, Stephen J. Solarz, wrote in 1995 for a journal article:

The disintegration of the Soviet Union, and the subsequent elimination of the rivalry between East and

West, strongly suggest that the survival of the communist regime in the North can no longer be taken for granted.[12]

Going a step further, Solarz offered prospects for Korean reunification. Highlighting that the North Korean regime was now at its final stage, he continued:

Similarly, just as the collapse of communism in East Germany was a necessary condition for the reunification of the two Germanys, the demise of communism in North Korea must now be considered a prerequisite for the reunification of the Korean peninsula. Indeed, if the precise date for the collapse of communism in North Korea cannot be predicted, the terminal status of the regime in Pyongyang can now be assumed.[13]

The views of many other analysts, policy makers, and politicians were in line with those of Solarz. They had offered a scenario like the following as to the fate of the Kim dynasty for a considerable time:

The North Korean government will go the way of East German Communism. Just as the seemingly impregnable Honecker regime rapidly disintegrated along with the Berlin Wall in November 1989, the Kim dynasty in North Korea has been expected to collapse at any minute.[14]

However, "this minute, of course, has lasted for more than two decades,"[15] defying all the predictions by experts about North Korea's impending fall, as if the observation by internationally bestselling American author and physician Tess Gerritsen were right. She said, "Evil doesn't die. It never dies. It just takes on a new face, a new name."[16] Its survival is not the whole story. It has grown like a deadly poisonous mushroom, posing even graver threat to the security and peace of the whole global community, especially of East Asia and the United States.

When Germany achieved reunification of the country in 1990, many South Koreans, including scholars, politicians, journalists, and business people, wasted no time in envisaging a Korean reunification similar to the German experience. Such an imagination proved wrong soon. Their euphoria was obvious in their travel to unified Germany, and the lectures and seminars held in Seoul to address the German experience of reunification and its implications for the Korean Peninsula, to which many Germans were invited.[17] However, the Korean Peninsula is very different from Germany, as follows:

First, East Germany and all other Eastern European communist countries were under the political, ideological, and military sphere of the Soviet Empire. It is simply unthinkable that any communist regime of the member countries of the Eastern Bloc—the Soviet Union, Poland, East Germany, Albania, Bulgaria, Yugoslavia, Romania, Czechoslovakia, and Hungary, all of which were on board the USSR could survive when the boat USSR sank under its own weight—communist totalitarianism, command economy, and excessive military expenditures. North Korea, notwithstanding being a communist state, was not an Eastern Bloc member and not a part of the unified force led by the USSR. It would be silly to ask passengers why they were not dead when the boat turned over, if they were not on board. Other communist regimes besides the North's—those of China, Cuba, Laos, and Vietnam—could also survive because they were not on the ferry USSR. While consolidating his leadership at home, Kim Il-sung could maintain even a balancing act between China and the Soviet Union, despite the fact that the two communist powers were North Korea's most important markets and major suppliers of oil and other basic necessities until the early 1990s.

Second, North Korea has tried its best to strengthen its ties with China, especially since the new Russian government under Boris Yeltsin refused to provide support for North Korea in 1992 and Beijing established diplomatic relations with South Korea in August of the same year. As for the strategic partnership between China and the USSR, the predecessor state to Russia, already in the 1950s and the 1960s, Beijing-Moscow relations became deeply strained following the Sino-Soviet Split (1956–1966), culminating in the undeclared Sino-Soviet border military conflict that lasted seven months in 1969. Since then the two colossal communist countries had competed fiercely with each other until they could dramatically improve bilateral relations after the dissolution of the Soviet Union and the establishment of the Russian Federation in 1991. Around this time, China's pro-market economy or "socialist market economy" was growing fast, and Russia was turning to privatization in a manner even more unregulated than China's, forming capitalist economic identity with China. In 1992, the two countries declared that they were pursuing a "constructive partnership." In 1996, they progressed toward a "strategic partnership," and in 2001, they signed a treaty of "friendship and cooperation." For North Korea as China's ally, the Sino-Russia treaty was encouraging as the two countries were expected to jointly serve its interest.

Third, since the Soviet dissolution, the connectivity between China and North Korea has steadily grown despite North Korea's unwavering nuclear ambition and reluctance to reform its economy, which has resulted in an increase in China's aid to North Korea. Overall, up to the present, China has remained the most decisive factor for the survival of the North's Kim dynasty. The specter of North Korean refugee exodus into China and other reasons, which will be elaborated later, have been among the major reasons for China's generous economic support for North Korea, often putting to shame even the United Nations Security Council (UNSC) sanctions on North Korea, with which China itself has agreed.[18]

Looking back, China has had political and cultural influence for thousands of years on the entire Korean Peninsula. Up until the late nineteenth century, Korea was a vassal state of China. During the Korean War in particular, the communist Chinese shed blood profusely for the North's Kim dynasty regime.[19] As a result, Sino-North Korean relationship was bonded by blood during the war. By contrast, the Soviet Union was officially just a sympathetic bystander in the Korean War.[20] Interestingly enough, with Beijing-Pyongyang relations getting closer, China, which has become rich thanks to "capitalism," has been feeding the Stalinist Kim dynasty regime of the North, which has gone bankrupt due to anti-capitalism or the command economy.

Considering all the drastic differences between Germany and the Korean Peninsula, it would be too naïve to link a Korean reunification with the German experience. Unified Germany has had considerable economic, social, and cultural problems after reunification due to the differences built up under the two different German systems. These German problems may have some implications for the Korean Peninsula only when a unified Korea actually comes in the form of German unification, which, however, remains far off now, by a long shot.

When Kim Il-sung breathed his last breath, the tyrant passed his nuclear brinkmanship on to his son and dynastic successor, Kim Jong-il. The Kim dynasty, referred to in North Korea as the Mount Paektu Bloodline, has symbolized the weirdest, most anachronistic form of autocracy on the planet. In 2010, the *Economist* reported on the dangerous nature of North Korea's hereditary rule, which is not found in any other communist country.

> North Korea has long been one of the world's most unpredictable and dangerous states. It now seems to be entering a period in which it could be even more unpredictable and dangerous than usual: the possible handover of power from one generation to the next.[21]

In 2013, Clause 2 of Article 10 of the newly edited Ten Principles for the Establishment of a Monolithic Ideological System of North Korea stated that the party and revolution must be carried "eternally" by the "the Mount Paektu Bloodline."[22]

Notes:

1 "Korean War Casualty Information," Korean War Educator (2016), http://www.koreanwar-educator.org/, accessed January 15, 2016.

2 See, for example, *CNN* Library, "Korean War Fast Facts," *CNN* (2018), https://edition.cnn.com/, accessed May 1, 2018.

3 L. Stack, "Korean War, a 'Forgotten' Conflict That Shaped the Modern World," *New York Times* (2018), https://www.nytimes.com/, accessed January 1, 2018.

4 J. Pak, "The Real Reason Kim Jong-un Wants to Declare an End to the Korean War," Brookings Institution (2018), https://www.brookings.edu/, accessed September 17, 2018.

5 M. Bishop, "North Korean Ex-assassin Recalls 1968, When the Korean Cold War Ran Hot," *NBC News* (2018), https://www.nbcnews.com/, accessed January 26, 2018.

6 M. Mark, "Failed North Korean Assassin Assimilates in the South," *New York Times* (2010), https://www.nytimes.com/, accessed December 17, 2016.

7 Staff research, "Half a Century of Major North Korean Provocations," *USA Today* (2013), https://www.usatoday.com/, accessed March 26, 2013.

8 See, for example, The Times Machine Archive, "2 Americans Slain by North Koreans in Clash at DMZ," *New York Times* (1976), https://www.nytimes.com/, accessed January 12, 2018.

9 All South Korean media reported this remark by Park.

10 See, for example, M. Tran, "North and South Korea: A History of Violence," *Guardian* (2010), https://www.theguardian.com/, accessed May 20, 2010.

11 Staff research, "Half a Century of Major North Korean Provocations," *USA Today* (2013).

12 S. J. Solarz, "The Collapse of Communism and the Future of the Korean Peninsula," *Fordham International Law Journal* (Berkeley, CA: Bepress, 1995), Vol. 19, Issue 1, Article 3, 25–31.

13 Ibid.

14 J. Feffer, "Why North Korea Today Is Not East Germany 1989," *Foreign Policy in Focus* (2014), https://fpif.org/, accessed February 11, 2014.

15 Ibid.

16 T. Gerritsen, "Quotes," Goodreads (2018), https://www.goodreads.com/, accessed June 12, 2018.

17 As for the jubilant mood of that time in South Korea, see, for instance, K. Rhee, "Korea's Unification: The Applicability of the German Experience," *Asian Survey* (1993), Vol. 33, Issue 4, 360.

18 E. Albert, "The China–North Korea Relationship," Council on Foreign Relations (2018), https://www.cfr.org/, accessed March 28, 2018.

19 M. Chan, "China's Korean War Veterans Still Waiting for Answers, 60 Years on," *South China Morning Post* (2018), https://www.scmp.com/, accessed July 28, 2013.

20 H. Wada, *The Korean War: An International History* (Lanham, MD: Rowman & Littlefield, 2014), 298.

21 The *Economist* Group, "Next of Kim," *Economist* (2010), https://www.economist.com/, accessed September 23, 2010.

22 "The Twisted Logic of the North Korean Regime," *Chosun Ilbo* (2013), http://www.chosun.com/, accessed February 12, 2017

CHAPTER 4

NORTH KOREA'S NUCLEAR WEAPONS DEVELOPMENT PROGRAM (NKNP)

Nuclear weapons have become militarily obsolete.[1] Any person or organization that invests heavily in obsolete things will go bankrupt. So will North Korea—meaning the regime in North will fall soon. I would like to remind readers here what I said at the outset of this book that the Kim Jong-un regime will collapse due to its own nuclear weapons. For this reason, much of this book needs to deal with how the regime's persistent obsession with nukes has been unfolding and will lead the Kim Jong-un regime to its demise. As we will see later on, the North Korean regime has repeatedly cheated the international community on its nuclear development program. Kim Jong-il, who immediately succeeded his father Kim Il-sung in 1994 as supreme leader of North Korea, began to demonstrate how inhuman the Mount Paektu Bloodline is. Kim Jong-il inherited from his father not only tyranny but also the cunning to intimidate the whole world. Nonetheless, North Koreans have been forced to worship Kim Il-sung and Kim Jong-il in the tradition of personality cult that spreads through North Korean society.

At this point, we need to get back to the time line of North Korean provocations after Kim Il-sung's death, as a reminder of the continuing ruthlessness of the Kim dynasty. Kim Jong-il's first three years, 1994–1996, as the supreme leader of North Korea repeated the same pattern of continuing armed provocations that his father had set.

North Korean citizens paying respect to the statues of Kim Il-sung (left) and Kim Jong-il at the Mansudae Grand Monument in Pyongyang (Source: Creative Commons <CC> BY-SA 3.0)

In December 1994, North Koreans shot down US Army helicopter, killing one American.

In May 1995, North Korean forces fired on a South Korean fishing boat, killing three.

In May 1996, seven North Korean soldiers crossed into the DMZ but returned after warning shots were fired.[2]

North Korea's familiar provocations continued during Kim Jong-il's rule of next three years, 1997–1999. Seeing the provocations continuing, international experts lamented the fact that international law cannot be enforced against North Korea. International jurists have said that all Kims of the Kim dynasty of the North should have been tried for crimes against humanity, but the Hague-based International Court of Justice has no enforcement system for its decisions.[3] It will surely help the world better understand the North Korean regime character and the reason why the international community has reached the limit of its patience to see "the absolute worst" regime on earth[4] continue and is determined more than ever to end it. The international consensus has been that the regime character unique to North Korea has much to do with its imminent downfall. The major provocations of the Kim regime in 1997–1999 included:

> In April 1997, five North Korean soldiers crossed the DMZ in Cheolwon, Gangwon-do, and fired on South Korean positions.
>
> In June 1997, three North Korean vessels crossed into South Korean territorial waters and attacked South Korean boats. A unit of North Korean soldiers crossed the DMZ and were turned back in a firefight.
>
> In June 1999, several clashes between North and South Korean vessels took place in the Yellow Sea near the border between the two countries.[5]

On the face of it, North Korean provocations of the 1990s seem to be business as usual and unworthy of particular attention here. However, the North Korean violence against international stability was veiling a far more formidable ploy threatening world peace that was secretly evolving in the world's most reclusive state. A new world order was evolving in the wake of the fall of the USSR and Eastern European communism. The North Korean regime, undoubtedly getting more isolated and frightened than ever, had to find out all possible ways and means to survive the new world order—a reality that was most unwelcome to North Korea.

To continue tyranny over the populace internally and to keep on threats to the security of South Korea, the United States, and the rest of international society externally, North Korea became desperate to make rapid progress on a deadly program. It was the North Korean nuclear weapons development program, or the North Korean nuclear program, which is abbreviated as NKNP in this book.[6] The NKNP was not a new offensive program of the Kim Jong-il era in North Korea, of course, and was Kim Il-sung's wicked gift of military adventurism for his son. However, Kim Jong-il had thought he had to speed up its development for his survival and increased armed threat to his principal foes, South Korea and the United States.

The time line of the NKNP shows that the Kim dynasty's nuclear efforts have continued for more than six decades. It dates to 1956, when the Soviet Union began training North Korean scientists and engineers, enabling the DPRK to acquire basic knowledge to initiate a nuclear program.[7] After the Korean Armistice Agreement that was signed on July 27, 1953, between the United States–led UN forces for the South, and North Korean and Chinese forces for the North, Kim Il-sung tried to convince its wartime ally, China, to share its nuclear weapons technologies. Kim twice asked Chinese ruler Mao Zedong for help but was refused both times.[8] However, North Korea became, in 1956, a founding member of the Soviet-led Joint Institute for Nuclear Research (JINR), located in Dubna, 110 kilometers north of Moscow. This meant that Kim Il-sung could ensure Soviet support to his nuclear ambition.[9]

Kim Il-sung had continued to attempt to provoke a second Korean war. Kim wanted to start another war in 1965 and asked China to send troops for the war. Professor Cheng Xiaohe of Renmin University of China noted on October 24, 2013, citing China's declassified diplomatic documents:

> In 1965, North Korea's founding leader Kim Il-sung met China's envoy to Pyongyang and explained the inevitability of a second Korean war and requested Chinese soldiers. Kim told Chinese diplomat Hao Deqing that North Korea would soon wage war because there was no way to unify the Koreas without a conflict, wrote Hao in a note he sent to Beijing after his meeting with the founder of North Korea. The Great Leader also told China that South Korean people were struggling from intensified class warfare and Pyongyang had already prepared for war.[10]

Even earlier, North Korea asked the Soviet Union in 1963 and China in 1964 for help in developing nuclear weapons of its own, but was rebuffed.[11]

Around that time, Soviet leader Nikita Khrushchev failed in his attempt to install medium range nuclear missiles in Cuba, which created the Cuban Missile Crisis (CMC) of October 1962. Khrushchev's failure in the confrontation with US president John F. Kennedy in the CMC was a great defeat for the Soviets, which contributed to Khrushchev's fall less than two years later. Khrushchev had, thus, little enthusiasm to buttress Kim Il-sung's nuclear scheme.[12] In China of that time, Mao's political clout was weakening from the repercussions of the failure of the Great Leap Forward, which was an economic and social campaign the Communist Party staged from 1958 to 1962 and on the eve of the Cultural Revolution that lasted from 1966 until 1976. As a result, Mao could not afford either intent or capacity to brace Kim Il-sung's nuclear adventure aimed at the South.[13]

However, Kim had doggedly strived for nuclear capability for North Korea, while sustaining his plan for another war against the South. Ten years after Hao Deqing wrote the note about Kim's war plan, Kim Il-sung attempted once again to convince Mao Zedong to support his plan for a unification of the Korean Peninsula by military force, at a Mao-Kim meeting on April 18, 1975,[14] but failed. Considering all this, it is anything but unimaginable that the key purpose of his fanatical pursuit of nuclear capability for North Korea was to launch a second Korean war. During the Mao-Kim summit, Kim Il-sung stated, "Their (Vietnam's and Cambodia's) victories are the same as a victory for us."[15]

He then suggested to Mao that he wanted to unify the Korean Peninsula by force of arms, much like Vietnam was about to be. Kim apparently used phrases like "a common victory for both of us" as he tried to steer the conversation toward a war to unify the Koreas.[16]

It is true that the United States, on its own part, considered the use of atomic bombs during the Korean War. In November 1950, a few months into the Korean War, US president Harry Truman told reporters at a press conference he would take whatever steps were necessary to win in Korea, including the use of nuclear weapons.[17]

> Those weapons, he added, would be controlled by military commanders in the field. In April of the next year, Truman put the finishing touches on Korea's nuclear war. He allowed nine nuclear bombs with fissile cores to be transferred into Air Force custody and transported to Okinawa. Truman also authorized another deployment of atomic-capable B-29s to Okinawa. Strategic Air Command set up a command-and-control team in Tokyo.[18]

However, the nuclear Korean war that Truman had initially thought about did not happen. In June 1951, the atomic-capable B-29s flew home, carrying their special weapons with them. They had never entered the battle zone proper, and they had not been part of the US Far East Air Force (FEAF) Bomber Command's strategic bombing campaign.[19] Analysts have offered various views on why President Truman abandoned a nuclear Korean war. Some have suggested that the frequent differences between Truman and Gen. Douglas MacArthur, who supported the use of nuclear bombs against North Korea and China, played a part in Truman's abandonment of using atomic bombs during the war.[20] Truman finally replaced MacArthur with Gen. Matthew Ridgway as commander-in-chief of the United Nations Command (UNCOM). However, this notion cannot be well established since Truman's successor, Dwight D. Eisenhower, who served as the thirty-fourth president of the United States from 1953 to 1961, also considered, but ultimately rejected, using nuclear weapons in Korea. The bottom line is that no nuclear weapons were ultimately used in the Korean War.[21]

Cold War historian John Lewis Gaddis seems to have offered perhaps the most plausible view. According to Gaddis, who was interviewed about the Korean War for a 1999 Public Broadcasting Service (PBS) documentary, "American Experience: Race for the Superbomb," the role of the atomic bomb was undefined. "It's one of the biggest dogs that did not bark in the entire cold war," says Gaddis.

> There was no clear strategy worked out ahead of time for what the role of nuclear weapons in the limited war would be. You're talking about a war, particularly after the Chinese intervened, with peasants coming down mountain trails carrying everything on their backs. And this was simply not what the atomic bomb had been built for. The only way that you can make the atomic bomb credible is precisely by not using— by keeping it out there as a kind of mysterious, awesome force. That to use it would actually cheapen it somehow.[22]

Glenn T. Seaborg, the late Nobel Prize–winning scientist and chancellor of the University of California, Berkeley, advised ten US presidents—from Harry Truman and Dwight Eisenhower to Bill Clinton—on nuclear policy, and was chairman of the United States Atomic Energy Commission from 1961 to 1971, where he pushed for commercial nuclear energy and the peaceful applications of nuclear science. The Nobel laureate who was once listed in the Guinness Book of World Records as the person with the longest entry in *Who's Who in America*, wrote in 1970 in his book titled *Peaceful Uses of Nuclear Energy*:

> It is a compilation of remarks, and excerpts of remarks, that I [Seaborg] have made in recent years in an effort to bring to the public the story of the remarkable benefits the peaceful atom has to offer man.[23]

Kim Il-sung should have taken seriously the observations about atomic power Gaddis and Seaborg had offered. But Kim could never do, of course, thanks to his lasting desire to occupy South Korea by force and to threaten the South's allies, and his fanatical love affair with nuclear weapons themselves. Some analysts have also claimed that the US deployment of nuclear-capable weapons, called "Honest John," in South Korea in January 1958 should be to blame as equally as North Korea's obstinate pursuit of nuclear weapons development program.[24] At first glance, they seem to suggest an even-handed approach to the issue of the NKNP. Also, they may claim that the arguments they put forward can be validated since they are based on a US memorandum declassified in February 1972.[25] However, we need to reexamine their arguments at least in four aspects.

First, strictly speaking, it may seem true that the US introduction into South Korea of the Honest John might have violated the armistice agreement "especially since American officials could not establish that the North Koreans had deployed atomic weapons."[26] The agreement contained a provision that banned new types of weapons or ammunition to be introduced into the Korean Peninsula by either the United States–led UN forces, or the North Korean and Chinese forces. However, international politics is about realities, not about plausible logic. It is all too true that Kim Il-sung had never ever abandoned his aspiration to take South Korea by military force before and after the Korean War. This drive and the efforts of Kim to prepare for another Korean war had already violated the armistice.

Second, when it comes to military weapons, we must be able to tell offensive from defensive arms. The US Eisenhower administration worried about "the prowess of North Korea's Chinese-backed military."[27] This worry was backed up about two decades later: in two separate press conferences in April and June 1975, US secretary of defense, James Schlesinger, said that the United States would retaliate with nuclear weapons if the hostile North attacked the South, and that it would maintain such weapons in South Korea, making it clear that the purpose of the US deployment of nuclear weapons along with its armed forces in South Korea as well as Europe was defensive.[28]

On December 27, 1957, the American Embassy in Seoul proposed announcing the arrival of the atomic-capable weapons in South Korea, saying the news was "bound to become public knowledge."[29] UNCOM agreed, and at a press conference in Seoul on January 28, 1958, the arrival of the atomic-capable weapons was announced. This "public" announcement amounted to a "public" defensive warning to North Korea's possible attempt to invade South Korea again.

Third, the Korean War broke out only five years after the end of the Second World War. By the time the Korean War Armistice Agreement was signed, the United States had become war weary. It had every reason to do its best to prevent another war from occurring on the Korean Peninsula, with every means available, as Kim Il-sung was pursuing it.[30]

Fourth, the United States had a serious financial problem due to the Korean War. To reduce the financial deficit after the Korean War, it moved to reduce the size of US forces in South Korea that depended on US financial aid. However, South Korean president Syng-man Rhee opposed this plan. As the most economical alternative to defend South Korea from a second invasion by Kim Il-sung, the United States had to introduce nuclear weapons into South Korea.[31]

These four aspects contradict the argument as suggested by some analysts that the United States does not come to any future talks for North Korean denuclearization with "totally clean hands."[32] In short, they need to be better advised before they try to make such a presumable argument, which will certainly please North Korea that has made frantic efforts to build up its nuclear arsenal for offensive purposes.

Notes:

1 Concerning the consensus on this view, see, for example, J. Joyner, "Are Nuclear Weapons Obsolete?" Atlantic Council (2010), https://www.atlanticcouncil.org/, accessed March 5, 2010.

2 Staff research, "Half a Century of Major North Korean Provocations," *USA Today* (2013).

3 As for the crimes of the Kim dynasty against humanity in particular, see, for example, A. Fifield, "North Korea's Prisons Are as Bad as Nazi Camps, Says

Judge Who Survived Auschwitz," *Washington Post* (2017), https://www.washing-tonpost.com/, accessed December 11, 2017.

4 P. Bouchard, "The 10 Most Repressive Countries in the World—and the 10 Most Free," *Medium* (2018), https://medium.com/, accessed August 2, 2018.

5 Staff research, "Half a Century of Major North Korean Provocations," *USA Today* (2013).

6 I have coined the term NKNP to briefly refer to the North Korean Nuclear Program. It is not an established term that stands for the program.

7 D. Bolton, *North Korea's Nuclear Program* (Washington, DC: American Security Project, 2012). https://www.americansecurityproject.org/, accessed August 20, 2012.

8 R. Kalvapalle, "How Did North Korea Get Nuclear Weapons?" *Global News* (2017), https://globalnews.ca/, accessed May 13, 2017. Quoted in D. Oberdorfer and R. Carlin, *The Two Koreas: A Contemporary History* (New York: Basic Books, 2014).

9 R. Kalvapalle, "How Did North Korea Get Nuclear Weapons?"

10 A. Yoo, "North Korea Wanted Second Korean War in 1965, Says Chinese Scholar," *South China Morning Post* (2013), https://www.scmp.com/, accessed October 24, 2013.

11 J. B. Lee, "US Deployment of Nuclear Weapons in 1950s South Korea & North Korea's Nuclear Development: Toward Denuclearization of the Korean Peninsula," *Asia-Pacific Journal: Japan Focus* (2009), Vol. 7, Issue 8, No. 3, https://apjjf.org/, accessed February 17, 2018.

12 For the Cuban Missile Crisis and its political aftermaths on Khrushchev, see, A. Whitman, "Khrushchev's Human Dimensions Brought Him to Power and to His Downfall," *New York Times* (1971), https://www.nytimes.com/, accessed August 15, 2018.

13 For a similar argument, see, A. Yoo, "North Korea Wanted Second Korean War in 1965, Says Chinese Scholar."

14 "Kim Il Sung Wanted China's Support for Second Korean War: Summit Records," *Mainichi* (2016), https://mainichi.jp/english/, accessed September 1, 2016.

15 Ibid. The *Mainichi* article quoted Shen Zhihua, a history professor and expert in Chinese-North Korean relations at East China Normal University as saying so, based on the records of the Mao-Kim talks Shen obtained.

16 Ibid.

17 C. Posey, "North Korea's Nuclear Program," *Air & Space Magazine/Smithsonian* (2015), https://www.airspacemag.com/, accessed July 30, 2015.

18 Ibid.

19 Ibid.

20 See, for instance, W. McElroy and J. Stromberg, *The United States at War* (audio-book series): *The Korean War and The Vietnam War* (St. Peters, MO: Knowledge Products, 2012).

21 A. Durkee, "How North Korea Got Its Nuclear Weapons in the First Place," *Mic* (2018), https://mic.com/, accessed June 10, 2018.

22 Quoted in C. Posey, "North Korea's Nuclear Program," *Air & Space Magazine* (2015).

23 G. T. Seaborg, *Peaceful Uses of Nuclear Energy: A Collection of Speeches* (Oak Ridge, TN: US Atomic Energy Commission, Technical Information Division, 1970), 1.

24 See, for example, W. Pincus, "The Dirty Secret of American Nuclear Arms in Korea," *New York Times* (2018), https://www.nytimes.com/, accessed March 19, 2018.

25 "Memorandum of a Conversation, Washington, November 28, 1956," Foreign Relations of the United States, 1955–1957, Korea, Vol. XXIII, Part 2, Office of the Historian of the US Department of State (1956).

26 W. Pincus, "The Dirty Secret of American Nuclear Arms in Korea."

27 Ibid.

28 J. B. Lee, "US Deployment of Nuclear Weapons in 1950s South Korea & North Korea's Nuclear Development: Toward Denuclearization of the Korean Peninsula."

29 W. Pincus, "The Dirty Secret of American Nuclear Arms in Korea."

30 W. McElroy and J. Stromberg, *The United States at War* (audiobook series): *The Korean War and The Vietnam War* (2012).

31 J. B. Lee, "US Deployment of Nuclear Weapons in 1950s South Korea & North Korea's Nuclear Development: Toward Denuclearization of the Korean Peninsula."

32 W. Pincus, "The Dirty Secret of American Nuclear Arms in Korea."

CHAPTER 5

KIM IL-SUNG'S DETERMINED PURSUIT OF NUCLEAR WEAPONS CONTINUES

To recap, it is undisputed that the US deployment of tactical nuclear weapons in South Korea was "defensive." It has been one of the key US strategic goals in East Asia to denuclearize the Korean Peninsula. No fact could better explain this US policy toward East Asia than the US withdrawal of its last nuclear weapons from South Korea in 1991. After the pullout of the nuclear deployment, South Korea has been protected under a US "nuclear umbrella" that was designed to counter a North Korean invasion. Major Aaron C. Baum, a researcher at the Air Command and Staff College at the Air University in the United States, notes that "from 1958 to 1991, the United States stationed nuclear artillery, bombs, and missiles in South Korea to counter a North Korean invasion." Baum continues that "South Korean strategic culture has and will continue to play a major role in determining its efforts to counter North Korean nuclear provocation."[1] As for the US "nuclear umbrella" in particular, Hans Kristensen and Robert Norris, scholars with the Federation of American Scientists elaborate:

> During the Cold War, the United States deployed nuclear weapons in South Korea continuously for 33 years, from 1958 to 1991. The South Korean-based nuclear arsenal peaked at an all-time high of

approximately 950 warheads in 1967. Since the last US nuclear weapons were withdrawn from South Korea in 1991, the United States has protected South Korea and Japan under a "nuclear umbrella" using nuclear bombers and submarines based elsewhere.[2]

The US decision to discontinue the nuclear deployment in Seoul made it clear that the deployment was defensive and had no intention to attack North Korea. In short, "American tactical nuclear weapons were stationed on the Korean Peninsula for much of the Cold War, on call and ready to repel a North Korean attack."[3] The move also confirmed Washington's policy objective to denuclearize the Korean Peninsula. The US nuclear removal from Seoul, however, had seriously weakened only South Korea's deterrence against a North Korean assault on the South. As it has turned out so far, the US elimination of nuclear weapons stationed in South Korea has never discouraged North Korean efforts to develop nuclear weapons. The US move has rather contributed to encouraging North Korea to pursue tenaciously its nuclear weapons program aimed at overpowering South Korea's military capability.

At last, North Korea has come to have nuclear weapons. Pyongyang has conducted six nuclear tests—in 2006, 2009, 2013, twice in 2016, and in 2017. With the NKNP gaining momentum, worried analysts in Seoul and Washington called for the United States to redeploy tactical nuclear weapons to South Korea, especially in 2017, when North Korea conducted the sixth, most powerful ever, nuclear test on September 3, followed by launching of four ballistic missiles on March 6. The North Korean government announced that the sixth test was a hydrogen bomb test. However, other analysts argue against the redeployment idea, calling the worried analysts "defense hawks."[4] According to the "dovish" experts:

Doing so would provide no resolution of the crisis over North Korea's nuclear weapons and would likely increase nuclear risks. Redeployment would also have serious implications for broader regional issues because it would likely be seen by China and Russia as further undermining their security.[5]

Few, including "defense hawks," would disagree with the US goal of denuclearizing the Korean Peninsula. The redeployment idea aims at discouraging the NKNP and a Korean denuclearization at the end of the day.[6] The key issue is whether North Korea has real intention to abandon its nuclear program. To understand North Korea's persistent intention to develop nuclear weapons under any circumstances, we need to get back to the time line of the NKNP. The NKNP can be examined in four stages.[7]

As mentioned, the first stage of the NKNP started in 1956, two years earlier than the US deployment of "defensive" nuclear-armed Honest John missiles and 280 mm atomic cannons to South Korea. The year 1959, three years after 1956, was very significant for the NKNP development. A report released in 2006 by the Woodrow Wilson International Center for Scholars says:

> In September 1959 the DPRK and the Soviet Union signed a treaty providing Soviet technical assistance for the establishment of a North Korean nuclear research center, which created the basis for Soviet assistance in the construction of an experimental reactor in the DPRK. North Korea and the USSR sign a nuclear cooperation agreement.[8]

In 1965, the Yongbyon IRT-2000[9] research reactor reached a power rating of two megawatt (MW). In less than a decade, in 1974, the Yongbyon IRT-2000 research reactor doubled its power rating to four MW.[10] The first stage of the NKNP had continued until the end of the 1970s, during which North Korea increased its initial nuclear facilities. However, the four stages of the NKNP cannot be clearly differentiated from each other due to the continuance of the NKNP throughout the four. Between the late 1970s and the early 1980s, North Korea began uranium mining operations at various locations near Sunchon and Pyongsan in the North.[11]

North Korea embarked on the second stage of its nuclear program in 1980. From 1980 to 1985, North Korea built a factory at Yongbyon to refine yellowcake and produce fuel for reactors, which included the construction of new reactors, a radiochemical separation plant, and research centers that put North Korea on its way to producing nuclear missile prototypes.[12] However, throughout the 1970s and 1980s, tension simmered even between Moscow and Pyongyang as North Korea rejected attempts by the international community to control its nuclear ambitions.[13] The Soviet Union did not support Kim Il-sung's nuclear ambitions for military purposes. In 1985, around the time the US intelligence discovered a third, once-secret reactor near the North Korean town of Yongbyon, North Korea signed the Nuclear Non-Proliferation Treaty (NPT),[14] a multilateral agreement whose dozens of signatories have committed to halting the spread of nuclear weapons and technology and promoting peaceful cooperation on nuclear energy.[15]

Behind the North Korean ratification of the NPT[16] was the Soviet government under Mikhail Gorbachev who served as the last leader of the Soviet Union from 1985 until 1991. Gorbachev's primary goal was to revive the Soviet economy after many stagnant years of his predecessors' rule. Gorbachev initiated in 1986 a new policy called perestroika—meaning "restructuring," which refers to the reformation of the Soviet political and economic system. Subsequently, in 1988, the Soviet leader introduced another new policy called glasnost—meaning "openness," which was aimed at increased openness and transparency in government institutions and activities in the Soviet Union.[17] With Gorbachev's coming to power, the Soviet totalitarian system began to unravel. *PBS* reports:

> In 1989, Soviet control of communist governments throughout Europe begins to weaken, and the Cold War ends. Post-Soviet states emerge in Eastern Europe and Central Asia. As the USSR's power declines, North Korea loses the security guarantees and economic support that had sustained it for 45 years.[18]

It is not difficult to imagine that at the inception stage of Gorbachev's initiatives for Soviet reform, issues like Soviet military buildup, let alone Soviet military support to North Korea, could not afford to be the Soviet leader's primary concern. In fact, Gorbachev began to reduce aid to North Korea after 1985 in favor of reconciliation with South Korea. Shortly after North Korea acceded to the NPT, the Soviets committed to helping North Korea construct a nuclear power plant in 1985.[19]

Despite the international circumstances unfolding in disfavor of the NKNP after the collapse of the USSR, Pyongyang was going against the times. In 1990, the United States learned of new construction at a nuclear complex near Yongbyon. US intelligence analysts suspected that North Korea, which had signed the NPT in 1985 but had not yet allowed inspections of its nuclear facilities, was in the early stages of building a nuclear bomb.[20] Through satellite photos, the US analysts discovered that a structure had been built that appeared to be capable of separating plutonium from nuclear fuel rods.[21] The NKNP looked like a car going down a steep hill, with no brakes. In response, the United States pursued a strategy in which North Korea's full compliance with the NPT would lead to progress on many pending issues, such as a normalization of US-DPRK relations.[22]

The year 1992 was a bad time for the NKNP. In 1992, North Korea eventually came to lose its key ally, as Russian president Boris Yeltsin and his government that took power in 1991 after the dissolution of the Soviet Union announced it would no longer honor the country's 1961 treaty of mutual defense and cooperation with North Korea. On November 21, 1992, concluding a three-day visit to South Korea, president Yeltsin promised to put pressure on North Korea to give up its effort to develop nuclear weapons. According to a *New York Times* report:

> Speaking at a news conference with President Roh Tae Woo of South Korea, Mr. Yeltsin said Russia had already stopped supplying North Korea with nuclear technology and materials. Without Russian help, he said, North Korea would not be able to develop nuclear arms.[23]

Everything seemed to have gone bad for the NKNP after the fall of communism in Eastern Europe. Prior to president Yeltsin's disavowal of the NKNP, US sanctions on North Korea were also mounting. Apparently conscious of the rising international pressure, North Korea signed a safeguards agreement with the International Atomic Energy Association (IAEA). The North allowed in May 1992 the first inspections of its nuclear facilities. *PBS* reports:

> For the first time, North Korea allows a team from IAEA, then headed by Hans Blix, to visit the facility at Yongbyon. Blix and the U.S. suspect that North Korea is secretly using its five-megawatt reactor and reprocessing facility at Yongbyon to turn spent fuel into weapons-grade plutonium. Before leaving, Blix arranges for fully equipped inspection teams to follow.[24]

However, the tenacious Kim Il-sung was the last person to give up nuclear ambitions. North Korea's defiant pursuit of nuclear weapons capabilities was rising rapidly. On top of that, its long-range ballistic missile technologies were also making rapid advances.[25] The IAEA inspections that started in 1992 did not go well. From January 1993, the North Koreans repeatedly blocked inspectors from visiting two of Yongbyon's suspected nuclear waste sites and IAEA inspectors found evidence that the country was not revealing the full extent of its plutonium production. In the resulting crisis, North Korea shocked the world even more as it announced that it would withdraw from the NPT in March 1993. After eighty-nine days, North Korea announced it had suspended its withdrawal (The NPT requires a ninety-day notice before a country can withdraw).[26] In December 1993, IAEA director general Blix announced that the agency was no longer able to provide "any meaningful assurances" that North Korea is not producing nuclear weapons.[27]

The year 1994 was a dramatic year for the NKNP in many aspects. The Clinton administration adopted a carrot and stick approach to the NKNP. Washington warned in April 1994 that if North Korea reprocessed plutonium from fuel rods, it would be crossing a "red line" that could trigger military action. However, the Clinton administration indicated at the same time that North Korea's full compliance with the NPT would lead to Pyongyang's economic and diplomatic benefits, including a normalization of relations.[28]

Essential is a detailed look at the Phase 2 of the NKNP that roughly ran a decade, from the mid-1980s to late 1994, given the significant backdrops for the NKNP during this stage. What the United States should have done and should have not done during this period, especially in 1994 in particular in the context of US-North Korea deal, has been controversial.[29] The most part of the Phase 2 seemed auspicious for the prospects for discouraging North Korea's nuclear ambitions. Major events that had happened until 1993 can be summarized as follows.

> 1985: In December, North Korea joins the NPT.
> 1991: In September, the United States removes nukes from South Korea.
> 1992: In January, two Koreas agree to denuclearize the Korean Peninsula. In detail, the governments of North and South Korea agree to "not test, manufacture, produce, receive, possess, store, deploy, or use nuclear weapons," as well as ban nuclear reprocessing and uranium enrichment facilities.[30]

However, North Korea revealed its true colors in 1993. About a month before it made the shocking announcement in March that it would pull out from the NPT, Pyongyang rejected inspections by the IAEA. In June 1994, amid escalating tensions on the Korean Peninsula, Jimmy Carter became the first former US president to visit North Korea, where he met with Kim Il-sung. Carter's private trip to Pyongyang to meet with Kim Il-sung seemed to have paved the way for a bilateral deal between the United States and North Korea.[31] However, US domestic pressure from Republicans who opposed negotiations with North Korea was growing stronger before Carter's visit to North Korea. Confronting the heavy Republican opposition, president

Bill Clinton appointed Robert Gallucci to start a new round of negotiations. After almost four months of difficult negotiations, the United States and North Korea signed, on October 21, 1994, an agreement called "Agreed Framework (AF)" to end their dispute over North Korea's nuclear program. However, the accord kept secret many details of how it would be put into effect. Gallucci said the two sides had signed a separate confidential document that is more specific than the four-page agreement that was made public after its signing at the North Korean mission to the UN.[32]

Subsequently, on October 18, president Clinton approved a plan to arrange more than four billion US dollars in energy aid to North Korea during the next decade in return for a commitment from the country's hardline communist leadership to freeze and gradually dismantle its nuclear weapons development program.[33] With the accord signed with North Korea, Pyongyang would freeze its nuclear activities, renounce any ambition to become a nuclear power, and open up two secret military sites to inspection by international experts so they could determine whether North Korea already had nuclear capability.[34]

To elaborate, the objective of the agreement was the freezing and replacement of North Korea's indigenous nuclear power plant program with more nuclear proliferation–resistant light water reactor (LWR) power plants, and the step-by-step normalization of relations between the United States and the DPRK. The agreement halted North Korea's decision to withdraw from the NPT as part of the accord.

For the NKNP of 1994, the sudden death of Kim Il-sung was most dramatic. Kim died on July 8, 1994, weeks after he met with Carter, and was succeeded by his son, Kim Jong-il. Carter tried to broker a diplomatic solution to the crisis. While in Pyongyang, the former US president made a controversial television appearance in which he detailed the commitments he had extracted from Kim Il-sung. He told *CNN* that

> Kim Il-sung "has given me assurance that as long as this good-faith effort is going on between the United States and North Korea, that the inspectors will stay on site and the surveillance equipment will not be interrupted."[35]

North Korean leader Kim Il-sung meets with former US president Jimmy Carter weeks before Kim's death. (Source: Courtesy of the Council on Foreign Relations. KCNA via AP Photo)

Carter also announced that Kim Il-sung had agreed to go back to the negotiating table. Carter's statement, however, contradicted the judgment of the US intelligence community. Prior to Carter's meeting with Kim Il-sung, the CIA assessed in 1994 that North Korea had already produced one or two nuclear weapons, validating its earlier suspicion in 1989 that North Korea was making utmost efforts to make progress toward building nuclear bombs.[36] This indicated that Kim Il-sung would hardly come to the negotiating table with true intentions to give up nuclear weapons.

In no time at all, North Korea's new leader Kim Jong-il showed what he had to do to put into practice what he was apparently instructed by his father Kim Il-sung to advance the NKNP. During Kim Jong-il's era, the NKNP took a remarkable leap, although Kim Jong-il pretended to follow the demand of international society for Pyongyang's denuclearization for a brief period of a few months after he took power in July 1994. The last period of the Phase 2 of the NKNP runs about ten months, from December 1993 to October 1994. During this period, the NKNP, if anything, made progress rather than retreat despite the AF.

Under the AF, on March 15, 1995, the United States, Japan, and the ROK founded a unique multilateral body called the Korean Peninsula

Energy Development Organization (KEDO) to implement the agreement.[37] In short, the KEDO was aimed at ending Pyongyang's nuclear weapons program. The international consortium—headquartered in New York City with a multilateral staff—was run by an executive board consisting of representatives of the United States, Japan, South Korea, and the European Union (EU).

As North Korea committed to freezing its illicit plutonium weapons program and halting construction on homegrown nuclear reactors under the AF, the United States, in exchange, pledged to provide sanctions relief, aid, and oil, as well as two LWRs for civilian use. The agreement called upon the United States to supply North Korea with fuel oil pending construction of the reactors. Japan, the ROK, and the United States covered most of KEDO's costs, including all administrative costs. Japan and the ROK financed a major portion of the two LWRs, while the United States contributed to the cost of heavy fuel oil shipments and the safe storage of the DPRK's spent fuel.[38]

Quite a few countries also made financial contributions, besides the United States, the ROK, and Japan. They included Argentina, Australia, Brunei, Canada, Finland, France, Germany, Greece, Hungary, Indonesia, Italy, Malaysia, Mexico, the Netherlands, New Zealand, Norway, Oman, Peru, Philippines, Singapore, Switzerland, Thailand, and the United Kingdom.[39]

The AF, which drew huge international attention and a mix of expectation and skepticism during its four-month negotiating period, began to send negative signals from the start, however. Only five days after the signing of the agreement, on October 26, 1994, IAEA chairman Blix told the British House of Commons' Foreign Affairs Select Committee that the IAEA was "not very happy" with the AF because it gave North Korea too much time to begin complying with the inspection regime.[40] Speaking of the NKNP time line, around the time when Blix made this remark, the second stage of the NKNP ended. Blix made the statement only three months after Kim Jong-il succeeded his father as North Korean leader. This heralded that the NKNP was likely to pick up speed during Kim Jong-il's rule of North Korea, betraying the expectations of the entire peace-loving world.

Notes:

1 A. Baum, "South Korean Efforts to Counter North Korean Aggression," the U.S. Air Force Center for Strategic Deterrence Studies, Trinity Site Papers (August 2018), 1.

2 H. Kristensen and R. Norris, "A History of US Nuclear Weapons in South Korea," *Bulletin of the Atomic Scientists* (2017), Vol. 73, Issue 6, https://www.tandfonline.com/, accessed October 26, 2017.

3 K. Mizokami, "Everything You Need to Know: The History of U.S. Nuclear Weapons in South Korea," *National Interest* (2017), https://nationalinterest.org/, accessed September 9, 2017.

4 Ibid.

5 Ibid.

6 For an in-depth analysis of the pros and cons of redeploying U.S. nuclear weapons to South Korea, see A. Woolf and E. Chanlett-Avery, *Redeploying U.S. Nuclear Weapons to South Korea: Background and Implications in Brief*, a US Congressional Research Service report, 7-5700 (September 14, 2017).

7 As for a detailed description of how the North Korean nuclear program has evolved, see, B. Szalontai and S. Radchenko, *North Korea's Efforts to Acquire Nuclear Technology and Nuclear Weapons: Evidence from Russian and Hungarian Archives*, 1st ed. (Washington, DC: Woodrow Wilson International Center for Scholars "Timeline of," 2006), 3.

8 Ibid., 1–79.

9 The IRT-2000 type consists of six Soviet experimental reactors. See, *Soviet Nuclear Research Reactors of the IRT-2000 Type*. An unclassified report. AID Work Assignment No. 31, Report 6 (Cameron Station, Alexandria, VA: Defense Documentation Center for Scientific and Technical Information, 1963).

10 B. Szalontai and S. Radchenko, *North Korea's Efforts to Acquire Nuclear Technology and Nuclear Weapons: Evidence from Russian and Hungarian Archives*.

11 D. Bolton, *North Korea's Nuclear Program*.

12 A. Durkee, "How North Korea Got Its Nuclear Weapons in the First Place."

13 Ibid.

14 For the North Korea Nuclear Time Line from 1985, see, for example, *CNN* Library, "North Korea Nuclear Timeline Fast Facts," *CNN* (2018), https://edition.cnn.com/, accessed April 3, 2018.

15 For the time line since 1985, see, "North Korea Nuclear Negotiations 1985–2018," Council on Foreign Relations (2018), https://www.cfr.org/, accessed August 12, 2018.

16 A total of 191 States have joined the treaty, including the five nuclear weapon States—China, France, Russia, United Kingdom, and United States. For the details of the NPT, see, "Treaty on the Non-Proliferation of Nuclear Weapons (NPT)," United Nations Office for Disarmament Affairs (2018), https://www.un.org/, accessed August 14, 2018.

17 As for glasnost and perestroika, see, for example, "Glasnost and Perestroika," Cold War Museum (2010), http://www.coldwar.org/, accessed January 23, 2018.

18 "Chronology: A Decade-Long Overview of the Threats, Deceptions and Diplomatic Ploys that Have Shaped U.S.–North Korea Relations," *PBS* (2014), https://www.pbs.org/, accessed September 10, 2016.

19 A. Durkee, "How North Korea Got Its Nuclear Weapons in the First Place."

20 "Chronology: A Decade-Long Overview of the Threats, Deceptions and Diplomatic Ploys that Have Shaped U.S.–North Korea Relations."

21 W. Pincus, "N. Korean Nuclear Conflict Has Deep Roots," *Washington Post* (2006), http://www.washingtonpost.com/, accessed September 15, 2016.

22 "Chronology: A Decade-Long Overview of the Threats, Deceptions and Diplomatic Ploys that Have Shaped U.S.–North Korea Relations," *PBS* (2014).

23 A. Pollack, "Yeltsin Vows Curb on North Koreans," *New York Times* (1992), https://www.nytimes.com/, accessed November 21, 1992.

24 "Chronology: A Decade-Long Overview of the Threats, Deceptions and Diplomatic Ploys that Have Shaped U.S.–North Korea Relations," *PBS* (2014).

25 As for the current level of North Korea's nuclear and missile technology, see, for example, S. Tisdall, "How the Nuclear-Armed Nations Brought the North Korea Crisis on Themselves," *Guardian* (2017), https://www.theguardian.com/, accessed September 5, 2017.

26 "Chronology: A Decade-Long Overview of the Threats, Deceptions and Diplomatic Ploys that Have Shaped U.S.–North Korea Relations," *PBS* (2014).

27 Ibid.

28 For the situation when the United States nearly went to war against North Korea in the spring of 1994 and the developments that followed, see, for example,

F. Kaplan, "Rolling Blunder," *Washington Monthly* (2004), https://washington-monthly.com/, accessed May 30, 2004.

29 For an analysis of this kind, see, for example, A. Carter, "Examining the Lessons of the 1994 U.S.–North Korea Deal," *PBS* (2014), https://www.pbs.org/, accessed December 27, 2018.

30 "North Korea Nuclear Negotiations 1985–2018," Council on Foreign Relations (2018).

31 Ibid.

32 A. Riding, "U.S. and North Korea Sign Pact to End Nuclear Dispute," *New York Times* (1994), https://www.nytimes.com/, accessed October 22, 1994.

33 D. Sanger, "Clinton Approves a Plan to Give Aid to North Koreans," *New York Times* (1994), https://www.nytimes.com/, accessed October 18, 1994.

34 A. Riding, "U.S. and North Korea Sign Pact to End Nuclear Dispute."

35 "Chronology: A Decade-Long Overview of the Threats, Deceptions and Diplomatic Ploys that Have Shaped U.S.–North Korea Relations," *PBS* (2014).

36 W. Pincus, "N. Korean Nuclear Conflict Has Deep Roots."

37 "The U.S.–North Korean Agreed Framework at a Glance," Arms Control Association (2018), https://www.armscontrol.org/, accessed July 30, 2018.

38 "Korean Peninsula Energy Development Organization (KEDO)," Nuclear Threat Initiative (2011), http://www.nti.org/, accessed October 26, 2011.

39 Ibid.

40 "North Korea Nuclear Weapons Program," Search Beat (2008), http://history.searchbeat.com/, accessed February 25, 2018.

CHAPTER 6

THE NKNP MAKES RELENTLESS PROGRESS AND THE KEDO STAGGERS

The third stage of the NKNP started in March 1995 when the KEDO was launched. To sum up, KEDO's principal activity was to construct two LWR nuclear power plants in North Korea to replace North Korea's Magnox type[1] reactors. The original target year for completion was 2003.[2] The KEDO began to reveal problems even before it broke ground in August 1997.[3] On March 18, 1996, Hans Blix reiterated his concern of 1994. Blix told the IAEA's board of governors that North Korea had still not made its initial declaration of the amount of plutonium they possessed, as required under the AF, and warned that without the declaration IAEA would lose the ability to verify that North Korea was not using its plutonium to develop weapons. In October 1997, North Korea seemed to comply with the IAEA demand. The spent nuclear fuel rods collected from Yongbyon nuclear facilities were encased in steel containers under IAEA inspection.[4]

However, North Korea betrayed again the international hope for a nuclear-free Korean Peninsula. Kim Jong-il regimes' provocations in violation of the AF that followed KEDO's establishment melted away the international wish. On August 31, 1998, North Korea's first orbital space launch attempt occurred. A satellite called Kwangmyongsong-1 had been launched from a launch site in Musudan-ri, Hwadae-gun, North Hamgyong Province, by a Paektusan-1 "satellite" launch vehicle. Although the Korean

The core of the 5 MW Yongbyon Magnox nuclear reactor, showing the fuel channel access ports (Source: IAEA)

Central News Agency announced that the satellite had successfully been placed into low Earth orbit, no objects were ever tracked in orbit from the launch, and outside North Korea it was considered to have been a failure. This missile flew over Japan's main island of Honshu, causing the Japanese government to retract one billion US dollars in aid for two civilian LWRs.[5] US military analysts suspected the so-called satellite launch was a trick for the testing of an intercontinental ballistic missile (ICBM).

With the KEDO in trouble due to the unexpected missile launch with the obvious aim to attack countries far away from East Asia, including the United States, and IAEA's rising suspicion that North Korea was not willing to comply with IAEA requirements for denuclearization, North Korea agreed, on September 13, 1999, to suspend testing of long-range missiles following talks with the United States. In exchange, the United States eased economic sanctions for the first time since the beginning of the Korean War in 1950.[6]

As it turned out soon, North Korea's imposition of the missile moratorium was a ruse aimed at alleviating US economic sanctions and earning time and resources to advance its nuclear and missile programs. Kim Jong-il benefited from the easing of banking, trade, and travel sanctions. On several occasions thereafter, the United States has lifted sanctions on North Korea in exchange for a promise to freeze its nuclear program and dismantle parts of its facilities as noted. However, Pyongyang has consistently reneged on its pledges until today.[7] North Korea's efforts for missile development alone testify enough to the constant lies and bad behavior of the Kim dynasty. As of November 30, 2017, North Korea had carried out one hundred seventeen tests of strategic missiles since its first such test in 1984.[8] Fifteen tests were performed under the rule of Kim Il-sung and sixteen under Kim Jong-il.[9] Under incumbent North Korean leader Kim Jong-un, more than eighty tests have been undertaken.[10]

Earlier in 1998, ironically, Kim Jong-il came to earn a significant financial help for the NKNP from none other than his archenemy, South Korea. Kim Dae-jung assumed the presidency of South Korea that year. Kim adopted the so-called Sunshine Policy,[11] which was the theoretical basis for South Korea's policy toward North Korea. The policy continued during his five-year term in office. Kim's successor, President Roh Moo-hyun, inherited Kim Dae-jung's engagement policy in 2003, which continued for another five years of his presidency. Kim and Roh have been known as the most liberal, left-wing presidents in modern history of South Korea.

On June 13–15, 2000, South Korean president Kim Dae-jung met with North Korean leader Kim Jong-il in Pyongyang for the first summit between Korean leaders since the peninsula's division five decades prior. The two leaders announced the June 15th South-North Joint Declaration as a result of the summit. The rapprochement resulted in several joint commercial and cultural projects, including construction of an industrial complex in North Korea and the reunification of families separated during the war. As the inter-Korean summit seemed to mean South-North reconciliation that could lower nuclear tensions with the world, the United States eased sanctions against the North further following the summit, allowing some trade and investment. Kim Dae-jung received the Nobel Peace Prize for successfully arranging the historic summit.

In October 2000, Washington and Pyongyang hosted goodwill trips. North Korean Gen. Jo Myong-rok met with US president Bill Clinton in Washington, making Jo the highest-ranking North Korean official to visit the United States. A few weeks later, US secretary of state Madeleine Albright traveled to North Korea to discuss the country's ballistic missile program and missile technology exports. The diplomatic overtures led to missile talks in November, but Clinton's presidency ended in early 2001 without making additional nuclear or missile deals.[12]

In January 2001, George W. Bush took office as US president and pursued a harder line toward Pyongyang with good reason. By that time North Korea had showed no signs of dismantling or even slowing down its nuclear and missile programs. On January 29, 2002, in his State of the Union address, President Bush characterized North Korea, along with Iraq and Iran, as part of an "axis of evil" and imposed new sanctions. President Bush denounced North Korea for aiming to threaten the peace of the world and posing a grave danger.[13] In April 2002, President Bush stated in a memorandum that the United States would not certify North Korea's compliance with the AF, due to a rocket test and missile-related transfers to Iran.[14]

The decade-long Sunshine Policy or engagement policy cost South Korea 4.5 billion US dollars. Despite the huge cost, the policy did not change North Korea's hostile policies toward South Korea and the rest of international society. *CNN* reported as follows on November 19, 2010, based on an annual white paper published by Seoul's Ministry of Unification, which the *Chosun Ilbo* newspaper in Seoul quoted:

> "Despite outward development over the past decade, inter-Korean relations have been under criticism from the public in terms of quality and process," the *Chosun Ilbo* newspaper quoted the white paper as saying. "They have in fact become increasingly disillusioned with the North and more worried about security as

the North continued its nuclear arms program." The sinking of the South Korean warship, the *Cheonan*, which killed 46 sailors earlier this year, showed that the North is ". . . consistently maintaining a reunification doctrine based on a strategy to turn the entire Korean Peninsula communist despite its outward policy in favor of cooperation and reconciliation."[15]

Mathematically, the price of the Sunshine Policy estimated at 4.5 billion US dollars at the 2005 value amounted to a production cost of over 3,000 nuclear weapons in 2015. Robert Alvarez, a senior scholar at the Institute for Policy Studies said in 2015 in his *Bulletin of the Atomic Scientists* column that the average annual per-unit nuclear weapon cost was about 1.8 million US dollars.[16] *CNBC* also reported in 2017:

> "South Korean government analysis has put North Korea's nuclear spending at $1.1 billion to $3.2 billion overall," reported Reuters last year, "although experts say it is impossible to make an accurate calculation given the secrecy surrounding the program, and estimates vary widely."[17]

North Korea began to defy outright Kim Dae-jung government's engagement policy. In fact, the June 15th South-North Joint Declaration, despite its superficial impression of entente, did not include any words about the NKNP, although Pyongyang's nuclear weapons development was of utmost concern for South Korea, the United States, and the rest of international society. The five-point joint statement, whose gist can be summarized as follows, failed to mention anything about denuclearizing North Korea.

1. The South and the North have agreed to resolve the question of reunification autonomously and through the joint efforts of the Korean people.

2. For the achievement of reunification, we have agreed that there is a common element in the South's concept of a confederation and the North's plan for a loose form of federation.

3. The South and the North have agreed to quickly settle humanitarian issues such as exchange visits by separated family members and relatives.

4. The South and the North have agreed to enhance mutual trust by promoting balanced development of the national economy.

5. The South and the North have agreed to hold a dialogue between relevant authorities soon to implement the above agreements.[18]

When it comes to the main concern of denuding North Korea, the Joint Declaration was nothing but a piece of empty bombast. It reminded the world of the slogan in 1984 of US presidential candidate Walter Mondale. Mondale's catchphrase "Where's the beef?" which he borrowed from an American international fast food restaurant chain, Wendy's, questioned the substance of the ideas his rival Gary Hart offered. As far as the denuclearization of the Korean Peninsula was concerned, the June 15 declaration was a huge step backward from the South-North Joint Declaration on the Denuclearization of the Korean Peninsula signed between the ROK and the DPRK some eight years earlier, on January 20, 1992. Despite all the fanfare, the Kim Dae-jung-Kim Jong-il summit was a "hamburger without the beef." The first four clauses of the six-clause Joint Declaration on the Korean denuclearization of 1992 read:

1. The South and the North shall not test, manufacture, produce, receive, possess, store, deploy, or use nuclear weapons.

2. The South and the North shall use nuclear energy solely for peaceful purposes.

3. The South and the North shall not possess nuclear reprocessing and uranium enrichment facilities.

4. The South and the North, in order to verify the denuclearization of the Korean peninsula, shall conduct inspection of the objects selected by the other side and agreed upon between the two sides,

in accordance with procedures and methods to be determined by the South-North Joint Nuclear Control Commission.[19]

The Joint Nuclear Control Commission as specified in Clause 4 of the agreement was created, and held thirteen meetings in 1992 and 1993, but they failed to produce any agreement that took effect. To elaborate, the last meeting was held in April 1993.[20] Clause 6 of the agreement read, "This Joint Declaration shall enter into force as of the day the two sides exchange appropriate instruments following the completion of their respective procedures for bringing it into effect."[21] Consequent to this clause of the declaration, the agreement never entered into force.[22] It is certainly legitimate to argue that South Korean president Kim Dae-jung should have learned from this failure of the past to avoid a declaration that failed to mention anything about the denuclearization of the Korean Peninsula.

For Kim Jong-il, the June 15 joint statement was nothing but a piece of worthless rhetoric in terms of a real denuclearization of the Korean Peninsula. He might have mocked the Joint Declaration that he himself signed but must have rejoiced at the prospect that the declaration would mean a great economic boost to the NKNP, as South Korea was expected to provide the North with lavish economic aid in the name of the Sunshine Policy that would immensely help Kim Jong-il advance his nuclear goals. In fact, Kim Jong-il's expectation was to materialize soon enough.

In early 2002, or about one-and-a-half years after the Joint Declaration, US intelligence sources revealed that North Korea secretly started the erection of a uranium enrichment facility at the Kangson site located in Chollima-guyok, just outside of Pyongyang. North Korea's centrifuge program was pursuing technology for a uranium enrichment program, which would produce material for nuclear weapons.[23] As the Kangson site designed to produce Uranium-235 heralded, the year 2002 registered from its onset a lot of events related to the advancement of the NKNP.[24] However, North Korea used a two-faced ploy consisting of disguised pursuit of nuclear weapons development on a consistent basis and seeming cooperation with international society trying to dismantle the NKNP. In other words, the DPRK was cheating South Korea, the United States, and the rest of the international community on its nuclear weapons development efforts with conciliatory gestures as it had made during the negotiations for the AF.

On July 2, 2002, twenty-five North Korean officials attended a training session in Seoul on safety management of the two LWRs under construction in Kumho, North Korea, as part of KEDO programs. The training session was held at a time when the ROK and the DPRK were on high alert following the inter-Korean naval clash on June 20. On July 20, the first direct flight between Sondok Airport in the DPRK and Yangyang Airport in the ROK was made possible thanks to the cooperation between the KEDO and the DPRK.[25]

> The air service would be used on a contingency basis, including for emergency medical evacuation, and would complement the current sea route between Sokcho (ROK) and Yangwha (DPRK) ports. The sea route was used to transport KEDO personnel and materials to and from the LWR project site in Kumho. On August 7, 2001, the KEDO held a ceremony to commemorate the pouring of the "first concrete" for the foundations of the main power plant buildings in Kumho. During the ceremony, the US delegate said that the ceremony offered clear evidence the United States and the KEDO were fulfilling their obligations regarding the reactor project and called on the DPRK to accept (IAEA) inspections.[26]

The "first concrete" pouring as late as 2001 at the construction site of the light water nuclear power plants being built by the KEDO meant the construction of two reactors was many years behind the original target completion year of 2003 under the 1994 agreement in Geneva. As we have seen so far, the delay was due to North Korea's continuing violations of the Geneva agreement.

On September 16, 2002, the United States revealed the DPRK's own admission that it had a secret nuclear weapons program in violation of the 1994 AF. The DPRK also informed the United States in October 2002 that it was no longer bound by the Framework. In late October, the EU Parliament, disturbed by North Korea's violation of the framework, also decided it would withhold its 2003 funding to the KEDO at least for now, if not permanently.[27]

All told, by early November 2002, the KEDO practically collapsed. Not only the three key players of the Geneva deal—the United States, the ROK, and Japan—but also the EU, concerned about international security, made a serious issue of the NKNP and KEDO's failure to make progress due to North Korea's reluctance to comply with the AF. On November 7, the EU Parliament adopted a nonbinding resolution to review the KEDO project.

The EU Parliament called on the DPRK to "take immediate steps" to comply with the nonproliferation regime and abandon its nuclear weapons program "in a verifiable manner," condemning it as a "serious breach" of its commitments under treaties such as the 1994 Agreed Framework.[28]

Notes:

1 There are six types of nuclear reactors, including Magnox. See, for example, *Nuclear Reactor Types* (London: Institution of Electrical Engineers, 2005). "Magnox reactors (see Fig 1.1(a)) were built in the UK from 1956 to 1971 but have now been superseded. The Magnox reactor is named after

the magnesium alloy used to encase the fuel, which is natural uranium metal." Like most other "Generation I nuclear reactors," the Magnox was designed with the dual purpose of producing electrical power and plutonium-239 for the nascent nuclear weapons program in Britain.

2 Stanley Foundation, *What Did We Learn From KEDO?* (Muscatine, IA: Stanley Foundation, 2006), 3.

3 "North Korea Nuclear Negotiations 1985–2018," Council on Foreign Relations (2018).

4 R. Alvarez, "North Korea: No Bygones at Yongbyon," *Bulletin of the Atomic Scientists* (2003), https://thebulletin.org/, accessed February 20, 2015.

5 "North Korea's Ballistic Missile Program," Center for Nonproliferation Studies (1998), http://cns.miis.edu/, accessed January 12, 2018.

6 "North Korea Nuclear Negotiations 1985–2018," Council on Foreign Relations (2018).

7 E. Albert, "What to Know about the Sanctions on North Korea," Council on Foreign Relations (2018), https://www.cfr.org/, accessed January 3, 2018.

8 "The CNS North Korea Missile Test Database," James Martin Center for Nonproliferation Studies (2017), https://www.nti.org/, accessed November 30, 2017.

9 S. Cotton, "Understanding North Korea's Missile Tests," James Martin Center for Nonproliferation Studies (2017), https://www.nti.org/, accessed December 20, 2017.

10 S. Choe and D. Sanger, "North Korea Fires Missile over Japan," *New York Times* (2017), https://www.nytimes.com/, accessed August 28, 2017.

11 The Sunshine Policy is based on the Aesop fable of a warm sun forcing a man to divest his coat after a cold wind had failed to do so.

12 "North Korea Nuclear Negotiations 1985–2018," Council on Foreign Relations (2018).

13 See, for instance, "Text of President Bush's 2002 State of the Union Address," *Washington Post* (2002), http://www.washingtonpost.com/, accessed November 25, 2012.

14 "North Korea Nuclear Negotiations 1985–2018," Council on Foreign Relations (2018).

15 A. Salmon, "South Korea: Policy of Engagement with North Is a Failure," *CNN* (2010), https://edition.cnn.com/, accessed November 20, 2010.

16 R. Alvarez, "More Bucks for the Bang," *Bulletin of the Atomic Scientists* (2015), https://thebulletin.org/, accessed February 23, 2015. A. Salmon, "South Korea: Policy of Engagement with North Is a Failure," *CNN* (2010), https://edition.cnn.com/, accessed November 20, 2010.

17 J. Blumberg, "Here's How Much a Nuclear Weapon Costs," *CNBC* (2017), https://www.cnbc.com/, accessed August 9, 2017.

18 "South-North Joint Declaration June 15, 2000," United States Institute of Peace (2000), https://www.usip.org/, accessed January 20, 2017.

19 See, for example, "Joint Declaration of the Denuclearization of the Korean Peninsula," United Nations Peacemaker (1992), https://peacemaker.un.org/, accessed January 15, 2017.

20 "Joint Declaration of South and North Korea on the Denuclearization of the Korean Peninsula," Nuclear Threat Initiative (2011), https://www.nti.org/, accessed October 26, 2011.

21 Ibid.

22 R. Carlin, "North Korea Said It's Willing to Talk Denuclearization (But No One Noticed)," *Diplomat* (2016), https://thediplomat.com/, accessed July 13, 2016.

23 "The U.S.–North Korean Agreed Framework at a Glance," Arms Control Association (2018).

24 A. Panda "Exclusive: Revealing Kangson, North Korea's First Covert Uranium Enrichment Site," *Diplomat* (2018), https://thediplomat.com/, accessed July 13, 2018.

25 "Korean Peninsula Energy Development Organization (KEDO)," Nuclear Threat Initiative (2011).

26 Ibid.

27 Ibid.

28 Ibid.

CHAPTER 7

THE FINAL PHASE OF THE NKNP

C onsidering the importance and timing of the KEDO for a North Korean denuclearization, how it collapsed requires an additional in-depth analysis, which in turn reveals how tenacious North Korea has been for nuclear development. Nothing could better explain Kim dynasty's enduring attachment for nuclear weapons than the failure of the KEDO. Despite North Korea's constant violations of the Geneva deal, the United States and Japan and South Korea tried their best even to barely keep the KEDO in existence in the hope that North Korea might abandon the NKNP in return for the two LWRs and other international aid. This expectation turned out to be grossly wrong. The US policy toward North Korea until October 2002, the final year of the Phase 3 of the NKNP, could be called a policy of patience, which was running out to the point of extinction.

On October 16, Washington announced that North Korea admitted in their talks to a "clandestine nuclear-weapons" program. David Sanger wrote in an article for the *New York Times*:

> Confronted by new American intelligence, North Korea has admitted that it has been conducting a major clandestine nuclear-weapons development program for the past several years, the Bush administration

said tonight. Officials added that North Korea had also informed them that it has now "nullified" its 1994 agreement with the United States to freeze all nuclear weapons development activity.[1]

The North Korean admission meant Pyongyang had fooled the United States, South Korea, and all other KEDO participatory countries for eight years since the KEDO was established. On October 20, North-South Korea talks in Pyongyang were undermined by the North's nuclear program "admission." Subsequently, US secretary of state Colin Powell said further US aid to North Korea was now in doubt. The North once again adopted a tricky, mercurial stance. At one moment it defiantly defended its "right" to weapons development and at the next it offered to halt nuclear program in return for aid and the signing of a nonaggression pact with the United States. Pyongyang argued that Washington had not kept to its side of the AF, as the construction of the LWRs—scheduled to be completed in 2003—was now years behind the agreed schedule.[2]

In early November 2002, the United States told Japan and the ROK that it was considering freezing its provision of fuel oil to the DPRK in retaliation for the DPRK's failure to follow the Geneva deal. However, on November 11, 2002, Japan and the ROK agreed that the KEDO had played a part in discouraging the NKNP and confirmed their intentions to continue with the project.[3] Three days later, on November 14, US president George Bush declared that November oil shipments to the North would be the last if the North continued to fail to put a halt to its weapons ambitions.[4]

On the same day, KEDO's executive board members met in New York to discuss the implications of the DPRK's acknowledgment in October that it was pursuing a program to produce highly enriched uranium (HEU) for nuclear weapons. The agreements the board members reached included:

The condemnation of the DPRK's pursuit of a nuclear weapons program, which is a clear and serious violation of its obligations under the AF, the NPT, its IAEA Safeguards Agreement, and the 1992 Joint South-North Declaration on the Denuclearization of the Korean Peninsula; the requirement that the DPRK must promptly eliminate its nuclear weapons program in a visible and verifiable manner; the continuation of relations and interaction between the DPRK and the KEDO and the members of its Executive Board hinging on the complete and permanent elimination of its nuclear weapons program; and the suspension of heavy fuel oil deliveries with the December shipment.[5]

The agreements of KEDO's board members highlighted that future shipments would depend on the DPRK's concrete and credible actions to dismantle completely its HEU program.[6] Considering this, other KEDO activities with the DPRK were required to be reviewed. At the beginning of December 2001, the KEDO decided to postpone its planned executive board meeting scheduled for December 11–12 of the year to review the KEDO missions in North Korea until early 2003. This postponement reflected KEDO's hope to have more time to watch the DPRK's moves over its nuclear program.[7]

November 27, 2002, North Korea accused the United States of deliberately misinterpreting its contested statement, twisting an assertion of its "right" to possess weapons into an "admission" of possession. The last month of 2002 revealed North Korea's escalating efforts to advance its nuclear development program in outright violation of the Geneva agreement as manifested in the KEDO. The breach of the agreement had already made it clear that the North had no intention whatsoever to abandon the NKNP. The following developments in December 2002 testifies to this. On December 4, 2002, IAEA responded to a DPRK letter. IAEA director general Mohamed ElBaradei expressed the agency's determination to fully implement IAEA safeguards in the DPRK in accordance with a resolution adopted in Vienna by the IAEA

Board of Governors on November 29, 2002, but the DPRK rejected the resolution. On December 4, the IAEA director general made a statement:

> The DPRK rejects the resolution in familiar terms, attributing the nuclear crisis in the Korean Peninsula to a hostile policy towards it (the DPRK). The letter does not respond directly to the resolution's request that the DPRK clarify reports of it having an undeclared uranium enrichment program. Dr. ElBaradei reiterates his "deep concern" about the situation, his readiness to discuss all related matters with the DPRK, and his determination to implement the IAEA safeguards agreement with the DPRK fully, and as soon as possible.[8]

In the week starting from December 22, North Korea resumed its nuclear activities at an amazing speed to the great surprise of international society. As a result, the KEDO had gone seriously incapacitated. According to scholars with *Bulletin of the Atomic Scientists*,

> The North began removing monitoring devices from the Yongbyon plant. Two days later, North Korea began repairs at the Yongbyon plant. On December 25, it emerged that North Korea had begun shipping fuel rods to the Yongbyon plant which could be used to produce plutonium. The next day the IAEA expressed concern in the light of UN confirmation that 1,000 fuel rods had been moved to the Yongbyon reactor. On December 27, North Korea said it was expelling the two IAEA nuclear inspectors from the country. It also announced it was planning to reopen a reprocessing plant, which could start producing weapons grade plutonium within months.[9]

An IAEA press release on December 22, 2002, described in detail DPRK's actions to stop international surveillance on its nuclear activities:

> The DPRK has taken further action today to disrupt the operation of IAEA safeguards equipment at the Nyongbyong (Yongbyon) site. Seals in the 5MW(e) reactor's spent fuel pond containing some 8,000 irradiated fuel rods have been removed by the DPRK, and the functioning of essential surveillance equipment has been impeded.[10]

The press release expressed particular concerns about DPRK's refusal to go along with international efforts for nonproliferation and its disruptive actions against IAEA's ability to enforce safeguards. The press release continued:

> "As the spent fuel contains a significant amount of plutonium, the DPRK's action is of great nonproliferation concern and represents a further disruption of the IAEA's ability to apply safeguards in the DPRK," said the IAEA's Director General, Mohamed ElBaradei. "Such containment and surveillance equipment play an essential role in allowing the IAEA to confirm under the Safeguards Agreement with the DPRK pursuant to the Non-Proliferation Treaty that nuclear material in the fuel rods has not been diverted to nuclear weapons or other nuclear explosive devices."[11]

Many analysts would like to argue, even without hard evidences to validate their contention, that North Korea must have pursued a double-dipping from the KEDO project, the two LWRs, plus associated benefits, and the advancement of its secret nuclear weapons program. Seen in this regard, KEDO's incapacitation must have meant a considerable loss not only to South Korea, the United States, and Japan but also to North Korea as it reflected North Korea's failure to earn the two LWRs and other economic benefits for free.

Yongbyon Nuclear Scientific Research Center 5 MWe experimental Magnox reactor, North Korea (Source: Public domain in the United States, created February 14, 2008)

Towards the end of 2002, to North Korea, disappointed with the near loss of the KEDO project that it intended to use for its one-sided benefit, news of consolation came from the South. On December 19, 2002,

South Korean presidential election was held and left-wing candidate Roh Moo-Hyun won the presidency, defeating with a narrow 2 percent margin of victory Lee Hoi-chang of the right-wing Grand National Party. Lee opposed the Sunshine Policy and made much of the North Korean situation threatening South Korea's security. As for later developments in inter-Korean relations, Roh Moo-hyun had a summit with North Korean leader Kim Jong-il in Pyongyang in 2007. The two leaders vowed to resolve the nuclear issues and expand business cooperation by building new joint economic zones, which would mean South Korea's substantial economic aid to North Korea. However, the agreement at the Roh-Kim summit made little headway after the North carried out a series of nuclear and missile tests,[12] as will be elaborated shortly in the final phase of the NKNP.

In 2003, the NKNP began to move into the final stage, Phase 4, which runs up to the present. Following the completion of the Kangson uranium enrichment plant in 2003,[13] North Korea was making constant progress in nuclear weapons development. The United States, the ROK, and Japan, and the rest of international society could not afford to let the Kim Jong-il regime's nuclear brinkmanship go unchallenged. A US military "surgical" strike against North Korea seemed to have emerged as the only option.

As previously mentioned, in September 2002, the United States had called for the suspension of the light water nuclear power project, claiming that the AF had been violated.[14] The US move was legitimate as it followed the DPRK's own admission that it had a secret nuclear weapons program in clear violation of the AF. The United States, Japan, and South Korea decided to put off procuring major parts for the reactors as one way of dealing with the DPRK's nuclear weapons program.[15] However, South Korea remained reluctant to agree on the immediate suspension of the project, which it believed would harden the DPRK's stance and escalate the situation.[16] The ROK's position seemed relevant as North Korea's complete departure from the KEDO project could mean international society's letting the NKNP go as North Korea pursued. North Korea took further actions to jeopardize the AF and KEDO's existence at the outset of the Phase 4.

On January 10, 2003, the DPRK government declared "an automatic and immediate effectuation of its withdrawal from the NPT." It insisted that the national sovereignty and supreme interests of the state were being seriously threatened by hostile US policy. The DPRK subsequently resumed operation of a small, graphite-moderated reactor at Yongbyon and announced that it would resume operation of its reprocessing plant, which the AF had frozen.[17]

The DPRK's continuing pursuit of nuclear weapons program gave the hawkish in the Bush administration who had opposed the AF a reason to abandon it. Their basic position was that North Korea's violation of the Geneva deal deserved Washington's punishment by its abandonment at the US end. They must have determined that such initiative of desertion would embarrass North Korea and put the country's nuclear program in trouble as North Korea's ploy for a double-dipping toward the KEDO program would be seriously impaired. John Bolton, then-undersecretary of state for arms control and international security under President Bush, later wrote that "this was the hammer I had been looking for to shatter the Agreed Framework."[18]

However, the Bush administration had not yet opted for a hardline approach to the NKNP and favored further dialogue with North Korea. For KEDO member countries, it was not easy to suspend the decade-long project overnight. The sunk cost in financial terms alone would be significant. KEDO executive board members held a two-day working-level meeting about its light water nuclear reactor project in July 2003. They discussed technical problems that might arise from a possible suspension of the project, but no decision was made on the issue.[19] By this time, the NKNP had become one of the most serious international security concerns. The United States expressed a grave concern about the impact of North Korean nuclear crisis on world security. On September 15, 2003, US energy secretary Spencer Abraham made a statement to the following effect concerning North Korean nuclear crisis and its possible impact on other countries at an IAEA conference in Vienna:

> The world should learn from the DPRK crisis and work hard to prevent other countries from secretly developing nuclear weapons. We must deal immediately and effectively with any state seeking to exploit the NPT to its own advantage. We have seen what happened when North Korea took this route. We need to look at why North Korea was able to make so much progress on its weapons program in the first place. It makes clear that the DPRK precedent is unacceptable, and the non-proliferation regime can withstand serious challenges when member states are prepared to take firm and necessary action.[20]

With the US concern about the grave threat the NKNP was posing to international peace mounting, US president George W. Bush had obviously determined that it would be in the interest of world security to try his best to engage North Korea under the AF up to the last minute. On September 15, 2003, President Bush indicated he would spend 3.72 million US dollars to finance an international consortium charged with implementing the 1994 anti-nuclear deal with the DPRK, which was on the brink of going defunct. Bush said in a memorandum to US secretary of state Colin Powell that the money, already earmarked in 2003 spending bills, was vital to US national security interests. But he made it clear that the cash would cover "administrative expenses only" of the KEDO.[21]

On September 24, 2003, President Bush decided to provide up to the 3.72 million US dollars to assist the KEDO for fiscal year 2003, but reiterated that no part of the contribution be used for construction of light water nuclear reactors in the DPRK. Bush also made it clear that it could not be used to finance heavy fuel oil shipments to the DPRK, which the KEDO suspended in November 2002.[22] The Bush administration had requested no money for KEDO in its 2004 fiscal year budget.[23] Consequently, the

KEDO had gone effectively defunct. Some events ensued as follows for the KEDO project but they were insignificant.

> On September 30, 2003, KEDO board members from Japan, the United States, and the ROK met for two days to coordinate policy to resolve the DPRK nuclear issue, but failed to reach an agreement on the suspension of the construction of the two LWRs. An informal KEDO board meeting held in New York on November 3–4, 2003, to discuss the same issue resulted in a decision to suspend the LWR project for a year-long period beginning December 1, 2003. A statement the KEDO board members issued on November 21 indicated that during the suspension, the various agreements and protocols between the KEDO and the DPRK would remain in effect.[24]

As the one-year suspension had already heralded, the year of 2004 had made little progress regarding the KEDO project. KEDO and DPRK officials had talks to discuss the suspension of the LWR project in March 2004, but failed to produce any plan for a possible resumption of the KEDO project. They signed only a memorandum of understanding, which ensured the safety of workers at the project site and confirmed that relevant agreements and protocols surrounding the project would remain in place.[25]

The outset of 2015, the second year of the LWR project suspension that was concluded on November 30, was seeing the KEDO breathing the last breath. It seemed as if North Korea wanted most to end the KEDO project as soon as possible. On February 10, 2005, North Korea declared that it had successfully manufactured nuclear weapons. Earlier in 2004, US intelligence agencies reportedly assessed that North Korea had anywhere from "possibly two to at least eight" nuclear warheads.[26] On December 8, 2005, the DPRK announced that it considered the LWR project terminated and declared that the KEDO no longer existed. The DPRK further stated that all KEDO personnel were to vacate the site by January 8, 2006, whereupon the DPRK would take complete control of the site. Concerning the DPRK's intention to take ownership of the site and all assets following KEDO's departure, the KEDO stated that it wished to repatriate all equipment at the site and seek compensation for its investments.[27]

> On January 8, 2006, the KEDO completed the withdrawal of its remaining 57 personnel left at the LWR project site. The DPRK refused to allow the return of approximately $44.5 million in construction facilities and equipment. KEDO's executive board decided to officially terminate the LWR project on May 31, 2006. South Korea was expected to shoulder the most severe financial losses. Of the 4.6 billion US dollars to be invested in the KEDO project, 1.56 US billion dollars had already been spent, with South Korea having made the lion's share of the contributions adding up to 1.13 billion US dollars.[28]

Different analysts have offered different accounts on the reasons of KEDO's failure. Some analysts argued that the KEDO project collapsed due to violations from both sides.[29] For example, a policy dialogue brief released in November 2006 by the Stanley Foundation in collaboration with the Weatherhead East Asian Institute at Columbia University tackled the reasons of KEDO's failure. Part of the brief noted that political problems surrounding the multibillion-dollar project created mistrust and slowed the implementation of the project and gave rise to North Korean charges that the United States was not serious about the implementation.[30] Such analysis may make sense, considering the complexities inherent in the nuclear development program North Korea had pursued over a long time until KEDO's final year 2006.

Nonetheless, KEDO's failure has given at least three important lessons to all countries involved. One is that democratic countries need to understand the quid pro quo principle would never work when they negotiate with an unpredictable, secretive regime, which, they have every reason to suspect, comes to the table only when it has hidden intentions and something to gain for free by cheating. Another is that it would be too difficult to dismantle a country's nuclear program to which it has already devoted so much effort, time, and money if it were not for voluntary cooperation of a nuclear-armed state in question. The third, which is by far the most important, is that it would be impossible to denuclearize a country prone to violating any agreement, which is the foundation of any negotiation, as amply demonstrated in North Korea's continued pursuit of nuclear and missiles programs even when the negotiation was underway, in violation of the AF that Pyongyang itself had agreed with. To sum up, the final stage, Phase 4, of the NKNP, which is currently ongoing, has marked the emergence of North Korea as a nuclear-armed state.

Notes:

1 D. Sanger, "North Korea Says It Has a Program on Nuclear Arms," *New York Times* (2002), https://www.nytimes.com/, accessed October 17, 2002.

2 "The Chronology of the North Korean Nuclear Program," *North Korean Review* (Fall, 2009), Vol. 5, Issue 2, 99–110.

3 "Korean Peninsula Energy Development Organization (KEDO)," Nuclear Threat Initiative (2011).

4 L. Paquette, *Teaching Political Science to Undergraduates: Active Pedagogy for the Microchip Mind* (Berlin, Germany: Walter de Gruyter GmbH, 2016), 49.

5 "Korean Peninsula Energy Development Organization (KEDO)," Nuclear Threat Initiative (2011).

6 Ibid.

7 Ibid.

8 "IAEA and DPRK: Chronology of Key Events," IAEA (2018), press release on April 16, 2009, https://www.iaea.org/, accessed June 15, 2018.

9 R. Norris and H. Kristensen, "North Korea's Nuclear Program, 2005," *Bulletin of the Atomic Scientists* (2005), Vol. 61, Issue 3, http://journals.sagepub.com/, accessed June 15, 2018.

10 "IAEA and DPRK: Chronology of Key Events," IAEA (2018).

11 Ibid.

12 H. Shin, "Factbox: History of Inter-Korean summits," Reuters (2018), https://www.reuters.com/, accessed February 10, 2018.

13 For Kangson uranium enrichment plant, see, for example, "Kangson Uranium Enrichment Plant Unzipped," *Analysans* (2018), http://analysans.net/, accessed July 15, 2018.

14 "Korean Peninsula Energy Development Organization (KEDO)," Nuclear Threat Initiative (2011).

15 Ibid.

16 Ibid.

17 Ibid.

18 J. Bolton, *Surrender Is Not an Option: Defending America at the United Nations* (New York: Simon and Schuster, 2008), 106.

19 "Korean Peninsula Energy Development Organization (KEDO)," Nuclear Threat Initiative (2011).

20 F. Murphy, "US Says World Must Learn from N. Korea Nuke Crisis," *NAPSNet Daily Report* (2003), http://oldsite.nautilus.org/, accessed September 25, 2015.

21 "US to Finance North Korea Nuclear Consortium," *NAPSNet Daily Report* (2003), http://oldsite.nautilus.org/, accessed September 25, 2015.

22 "Korean Peninsula Energy Development Organization (KEDO)," Nuclear Threat Initiative (2011).

23 "US to Finance North Korea Nuclear Consortium," *NAPSNet Daily Report* (2003).

24 "Korean Peninsula Energy Development Organization (KEDO)," Nuclear Threat Initiative (2011).

25 Ibid.

26 See, for example, J. McLaughlin, "Pyongyang's Growing Nuclear Arsenal," Wisconsin Project on Nuclear Arms Control (2017), https://www.wisconsin-project.org/, accessed March 1, 2017.

27 Ibid.

28 Ibid.

29 See, for example, "The Six-Party Talks at a Glance," Arms Control Association (2018), https://www.armscontrol.org/, accessed July 31, 2018.

30 "What Did We Learn From KEDO?" A policy dialog brief, Stanley Foundation (2006), https://www.stanleyfoundation.org/, accessed November 23, 2017.

CHAPTER 8

SIX-PARTY
TALKS WERE DOOMED TO FAILURE

When the AF collapsed in the wake of North Korea's withdrawal from the NPT in early 2003, the six-party talks took the AF's place as an international attempt to dismantle the NKNP. A total of six rounds of sporadic talks were held in China from August 2003 to September 2007 for multilateral negotiations. Within the six-party talks framework, China, South Korea, the United States, Japan, and Russia are five parties negotiating with North Korea. Although the talks were hosted in Beijing and chaired by China, the argument that China was the initiator and promoter of the talks[1] is not entirely correct. The East Asian security situation aggravated in early 2003 by North Korea's provocations, as well as its pullout from the NPT was the real initiator. At the onset of 2003, tensions heightened in East Asia. In March 2003, North Korean fighter aircraft intercepted a US spy plane over the Sea of Japan. This incident led the United States, North Korea, and China to hold trilateral talks in Beijing a month later in a prelude to the first round of the six-party talks.[2] The talks, however, have failed to achieve the ultimate objective of denuclearizing North Korea. The first four-year time line of the talks as summarized below is self-explanatory to the nature of the talks and the reason why the talks were doomed to failure.[3]

August 2003: The six-party talks start.

June 2004: The United States offers tens of thousands of tons of heavy fuel oil in exchange for a North Korean dismantling its nuclear weapons program but the talks break down in July.

September 2004: North Korea announces it has developed a plutonium-based nuclear device.

February 2005: The North suspends involvement in six party talks and admits publicly for the first time that it has produced nuclear weapons for "self-defense."

July 2005: Talks restart after the United States and South Korea offer electricity and food aid, but after thirteen days the talks are temporarily suspended.

September 2005: North Korea agrees to abandon all its nuclear weapons development in return for possible access to a light water civilian nuclear reactor.

In November 2005, six-party negotiations resumed but collapsed after just three days. The sudden breakdown of the talks puzzled the world for several months, but the reason for the collapse was soon to be brought to light in a series of North Korea's tests of weapons of mass destruction (WMDs) that followed. North Korea received substantial rewards for its fake moves to inactivate its nuclear activities.

July 2006: North Korea test-fires seven missiles including a long-range Taepodong-2 missile reportedly having the capability to hit the United States.

October 2006: North Korea conducts its first test of a nuclear weapon. UN imposes economic and commercial sanctions on North Korea.

July 2007: North Korea shuts down its main Yongbyon reactor after receiving 50,000 tons of heavy fuel oil as part of an aid package.

> September 2007: After further talks, Washington announces that North Korea has agreed to disable its nuclear facilities and give up plutonium stocks by the end of the year.[4]

Despite the seeming progress toward a dismantlement of the NKNP that had happened in July–September 2007, the six-party talks held between 2003 and 2007 could make little progress due to North Korea's disguised promises that it would disable its nuclear program.[5] For example, North Korea's shutdown of its Yongbyon reactor was nothing but symbolic and a bait to get fifty thousand tons of heavy fuel its flagging economy badly needed. What had happened after September 2007 testified to this. A final meeting was decided on before the end of 2007. However, this was never realized because of North Korea's suspicious compliance with the nuclear deal. The DPRK issued a report of its inventory in November 2007 and claimed that since it fulfilled its side of the bargain, it was waiting for the promised shipment of aid from the United States. However, Washington claimed the inventory list was definitely incomplete and until the complete list was given by the DPRK, aid would be suspended.[6]

By all accounts, North Korea kept cheating the international community on its nuclear weapons program during this four-year period.[7] From August 2003 to September 2007, North Korea could advance its nuclear program using international aid.[8] In only two years after September 2007, North Korea entered an era of earnest nuclear development as the following time line shows. It admitted in 2009 that it was capable of producing nuclear bombs. All told, the failure of the six-party talks was a forgone conclusion: The Kim dynasty regime has had no intention whatsoever to give up nuclear weapons.

> March 2008: North-South relations deteriorate sharply after new South Korean president Lee Myung-bak promises to take a harder line on North Korea.

October 2008: The North agrees to provide full access to Yongbyon nuclear site after the United States removes it from terrorism blacklist.

January 2009: North Korea says it is scrapping all military and political deals with the South, accusing it of "hostile intent."

April 2009: North Korea launches a long-range rocket. Condemnation from the UN Security Council prompts North Korea to walk out of six-party talks and restart its nuclear facilities.

May 2009: North Korea carries out its second underground nuclear test. UN Security Council condemns move in June.

November 2009: North Korea's state-run news agency reports the reprocessing of 8,000 spent fuel rods is complete, garnering enough weapons-grade plutonium for one to two nuclear bombs.[9]

Since the discontinuation of the six-party talks in 2009, North Korean provocations against South Korea and the international community, along with its nuclear weapons development, have become more outright and conspicuous. In March, 2010, North Korea sank South Korean warship *Cheonan* near sea border. In early November 2010, North Korea showed a visiting American nuclear scientist of Stanford University, Siegfried S. Hecker, a vast new secretly built facility for enriching uranium at its Yongbyon complex. The revelation sparked alarm and anger in the United States, South Korea, and Japan, and confronted the Obama administration with the prospect that the country was preparing to expand its nuclear arsenal or build a far more powerful type of atomic bomb.[10]

The disjointed process of the six-nation talks with no intended headway for a North Korean denuclearization is a reminder of the familiar North Korean negotiating variety that is characterized by sophisticated lying—participation in a negotiation to seek benefits and rewards for fake pledges and a walkout from it that was usually followed by

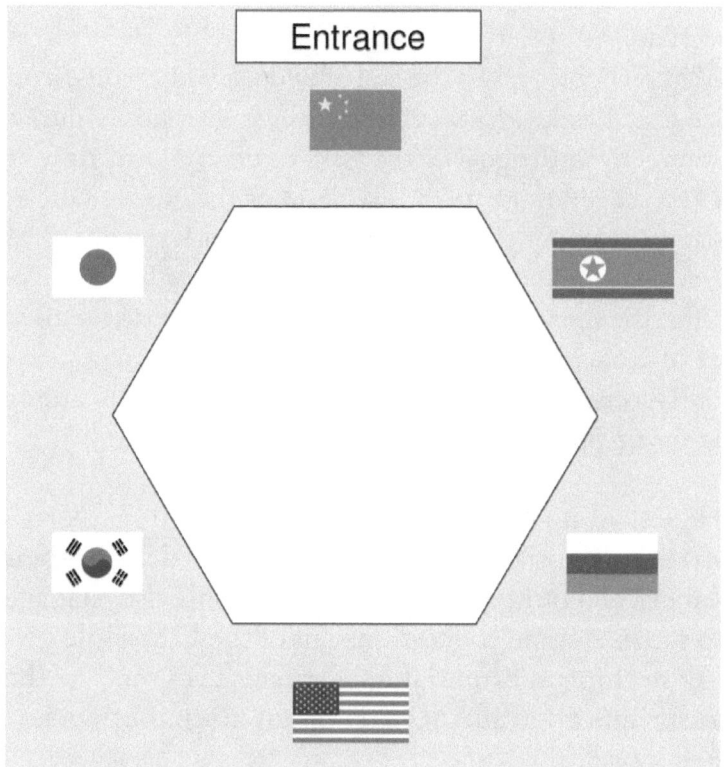

A figure of a table of the six party talks (Source: Creative Commons—CC BY-SA 3.0)

provocations, such as nuclear tests and long-range missile firings. For example, the US financial sanction on about twenty-five million US dollars of North Korean funds that was frozen at Macau's Banco Delta Asia (BDA) for illicit financial activities, including counterfeiting and money-laundering, was lifted in 2007 "to reciprocate the positive steps the North Koreans have taken towards freezing their Yongbyon nuclear reactor" but it was obvious that North Korea used the unfrozen money to build up its nuclear activities. In other words, the unfreeze of the illicit funds amounted to a reward for the North's recurrent fake promises of denuclearization.

Some analysts still say the talks "ceased" in 2009, but it is better advised to say the talks "ended" then. On April 5, 2009, North Korea proceeded with its announced satellite launch, despite international pressure not to do so. International society believed that the satellite launch was in fact a test of ICBM technology.[11] By the end of 2006, it had become a no-brainer knowledge that Pyongyang would never ever give up its nuclear weapons program. Given the goal of the talks to undo North Korea's nuclear program and the US estimate in early 2018 of the North Korean nuclear weapons at up to sixty,[12] the long-drawn-out six-nation talks were a grand failure. Analysts noted that the talks had only earned North Korea both the time and the money, such as the black money frozen at BDA, that it needed to advance its nuclear weapons program. *Time* magazine reported already on December 23, 2006, or three-and-a-half years after the talks began, on the prospects of the talks for 2007:

> Here's a no-brainer prediction for 2007: North Korean negotiators will spend the year driving their American counterparts crazy. They will also manage to squeeze some concessions out of the U.S. while giving nothing substantial away themselves, and in the meantime continue developing an arsenal of nuclear weapons.[13]

It is critical for the international community to remember the past again and over again as it should not repeat the mistakes it has made in dealing with the North. Toward the end of 2006, analysts already began to offer in earnest pessimistic views that a complete dismantling of the NKNP would be impossible. The then senior fellow at the Brookings Institution, Ivo H. Daalder, offered what might be considered an eclectic approach to the NKNP. Daalder said:

> A more realistic goal than a complete disarmament would be for North Korea to freeze and verify its existing program. This means: No more testing, a freeze on plutonium production, the return of international monitors, and the end of North Korea's uranium enrichment program.[14]

His view, however, was not so much practical as theoretical. In order to better understand the reason for the six-party talks' failure, we need to fathom the NKNP further. First of all, we need to understand North Korea's incurable obsession with nuclear weapons. The mania for nukes derives from the ruthless regime's long-standing *Songun* policy—the "military first" policy prioritizing the Korean People's Army (KPA) in the affairs of state and allocation of resources. The roots of *Songun* are traced to Kim Il-sung's guerilla activities, which are said to be marginal at best, if any, against the Japanese during the 1930s.[15] The *Songun* era began in 1960 when a young Kim Jong-il, together with his father Kim Il-sung, visited on August 25 one of major KPA installations in Pyongyang.[16] At the Fifth Plenum of the Fourth Korea Workers' Party (KWP) Central Committee in December 1962, Kim Il-sung put into effect the four military lines policy from which the *Songun* ideology was derived. August 25, the Day of *Songun*, is now a national holiday in North Korea. With the *Songun* policy placed at the core of North Korean politics, North Korean military doctrine shifted radically in December 1962 away from the doctrine of regular warfare to an expanded version that embraced people's war. GlobalSecurity.org describes in detail the key features of the *Songun* politics:

> Kim Il Sung espoused the Four Military Guidelines: to arm the entire population; to fortify the entire country; to train the entire army as a "cadre army"; and to modernize weaponry, doctrine, and tactics under the principle of self-reliance in national defense. The adoption of this military line signaled a shift from a Soviet-style strategy to a Maoist protracted war of attrition. Conventional warfare strategy was incorporated into and subordinated to the overall concept of people's war and the mobilization of the entire people through reinforcement of ideological training. These principles are formally adopted in Article 60 of the 1992 constitution.[17]

A more important feature of *Songun* is that this doctrine has amalgamated into the North Korean cult of personality surrounding its ruling Kim family that has existed in North Korea for seven decades and can be found in many examples of North Korean culture,[18] especially in the North's military culture. The *Songun* policy augments the philosophy of *Juche*, generally understood as *self-reliance*, which Kim Il-sung had developed in the late 1940s or the early 1950s as the dominant political ideology governing the North.[19] In the 1950s and 1960s, Kim Il-sung continued to develop the *Juche* philosophy as a variant of Marxism-Leninism until it became distinctly Korean in character.[20] All told, the *Songun* policy amounts to a key component of the North Korean cult of the ruling Kim family and reflects the dominant political philosophy, *Juche*, of the Kim dynasty. After Kim Il-sung's death in 1994, Kim Jong-il introduced in 1995 *Songun* as "a revolutionary idea of attaching great importance to the army" and as "a politics emphasizing the perfect unity and the single-hearted unity of the party, army and the people, and the role of the army as the vanguards in the wake of his first military unit visit for that year. This was a little shift from the government's previous guiding policy, Kim Il-sung's *Juche*,[21] but it is still rooted in Kim Il-sung's ideas and reflects the North's personality cult. In sum, the *Songun* doctrine exhibits the key feature not only of the North Korean military but also of the entire North Korean life and culture.

Naturally, the NKNP has been at the core of the *Songun* politics of the North Korean regime. In this capacity, it represents the key aspect of the personality cult of the Kim dynasty and North Korea's militaristic culture as well as the most powerful instrument to oppress the people. It has been well validated that culture won't change easily: it lasts "forever," especially in isolated societies, as seen in tribal communities in remote areas of Africa, Asia, and South America, where voodoo science is still being practiced. To restate, culture change has been considered extremely hard and one of the most difficult challenges to any organization, society, or region.[22] The difficulty or the near impossibility of dismantling the NKNP can be explained in a large part by taking a close look at the origin of the *Songun* politics and its evolution. This understanding must be the starting point in any discussion of how to dismantle the NKNP.

Analysts have generally noted that previous attempts to persuade North Korea to back off its nuclear weapons program failed amid the North's reversals and enmity between Pyongyang and Washington.[23] The expression "reversals" is misleading. The key point is that Pyongyang has never had any "authentic" intention to give up its nuclear program in return for US and South Korean aid, economic, political, or diplomatic. As for the six-party talks, the breakdowns and resumptions of the negotiations that had happened between North Korea and five other nations until the discontinuation of the talks in 2009 were dotted with North Korea's acts of defiance against the aim of the talks to find a peaceful resolution to the security concerns about the NKNP.

A closer look at the frequent turnarounds of North Korea reveals a tricky North Korean mode that has remained so consistent throughout its development of nuclear weapons that the term "reversals" is not suited to describing the NKNP. The steady North Korean pattern repeatedly shows the Kim dynasty has no intentions to abandon its nuclear program. The animosity between North Korea and the United States is also North Korea's own creation. Since the Korean War, it has been North Korea's hostile Kim regime that has repeated provocations against the United States and South Korea. No reasonable analyst could dispute this view that is based on facts. Regarding North Korea's decades-old lying to the international community, Nyshka Chandran, a writer for *CNBC*, says:

> For decades, the international community has tried to stop North Korea's nuclear weapon and missile development. It has failed. The pariah state has promised disarmament more than once, only to repeatedly backtrack on its commitments. It has duped multiple U.S. presidential administrations, each of which has passed the North Korea problem onto the next.[24]

Looking ahead, the international community must realize once again that any negotiation aimed at taking down the NKNP is very likely to play into the North Korean regime's hands, only to benefit the North's nuclear advancement program.[25] Evans J. R. Revere, a policy analyst with the Brookings Institution, declares:

> The US administration will soon meet the immovable object of a North Korean regime that has declared it will never give up its nuclear weapons "even in a dream." Those who have negotiated nuclear matters with Pyongyang know that Kim's words were a familiar North Korean demand to end the "threat" posed by the U.S.–South Korea alliance, the presence of U.S. troops in South Korea, and the nuclear umbrella that defends South Korea and Japan.[26]

Despite North Korea's dogged efforts for and deep-seated preoccupation with nuclear weapons development as the last thing it could ever abandon, it would not be totally impossible to knock down the NKNP, if a strong, unified international effort could be made. Unfortunately, the six-party talks have had an inherent contradiction. At first glance, the talks look like a tug of war between a coalition of five strong nations and an adventurous but fundamentally shaky state, whose outcome seemed to be foretold—an undisputed win for the coalition. The disappointing results of the talks, therefore, have puzzled the world.

In short, China has been a key factor that has contributed to the failure of the talks. China, as the key player of the talks, is to blame for leading the talks to a stillbirth. Despite the coalition's seemingly overwhelming edge over North Korea, it remained enervated due to China's lukewarm pressure on North Korea. The five-state coalition participating in the six-party talks could be compared with a house divided inside, that is, a league split between China and four other nations. Hwang Jang-yop, the highest-ranking North Korean defector ever to South Korea, had repeatedly emphasized until he died in 2010 that the future of North Korea was in the hands of China. Hwang would remark that a complete separation of North Korea from China only could demolish the NKNP.[27] Other analysts offered same views. The *Washington Post* reported on April 9, 2013, "The Holy Grail in North Korea diplomacy is getting China to put pressure on its long-time protege."[28] During the series of the tug of war, China was actually pulling the rope toward the coalition's rival, North Korea.

Since Pyongyang's first nuclear test in October 2006, the UNSC had passed eight resolutions for sanctions against North Korea over eleven years until September 2017 when Pyongyang carried out its sixth nuclear test. China has been long suspected of virtually violating the UNSC sanctions to which it has agreed.[29] China has often pretended to tighten its pressure on North Korea but has actually loosened the UNSC sanctions on Pyongyang, which Beijing has a six-decade-old defense treaty with until now. North Korea is China's only military ally in East Asia. China has long been the North's lifeline as a nearly single trading partner and key supplier of food and fuel. Other than China, no country has such an overwhelming economic, political, and military influence on North Korea. An odd dilemma facing the international community vis-à-vis the issue of dismantling the NKNP is that despite the fact that both the United States and China have agreed with the UNSC sanctions against North Korea, Washington has had to make extraordinary efforts to persuade Beijing to faithfully fulfill the UNSC sanctions against North Korea since China has not been faithful to implementing the sanctions. Beijing has been at least ambivalent about the sanctions against Pyongyang.[30] An *Atlantic* article describes this strange international quandary:

> The latest effort to counter North Korea's nuclear program—UN Security Council sanctions on several North Korean exports, orchestrated by American and Chinese negotiators—appears to indicate that the United States and China are finally joining forces to crush Kim's nuclear ambitions. Yet the unity of purpose fades upon closer inspection. U.S. officials have questioned whether the Chinese government

will enforce the sanctions, as the Trump administration considers ways to retaliate if Beijing fails to get tougher on its ally in Pyongyang.[31]

China has protected the only remaining Stalinist state in the world from collapsing. We need to dissect why China wants to help, rather than tighten its pressure on, North Korea. Two reasons have often been cited for Beijing's reluctance to put effective pressure on Pyongyang.

First, in Chinese view, Pyongyang serves as a buffer zone for China against US military presence in East Asia. China has long feared the United States would capitalize on the fall of the North Korean leadership by expanding American military influence on the Korean Peninsula.[32] Beijing's continuing tolerance of and aid to the North's Kim regime is a highly calculated strategic move reflecting the Chinese fear of US military presence in its vicinity. "From China's perspective, any substantial involvement of a 'foreign power' in its neighborhood would be seen as a potential threat."[33] This means that the NKNP can be a deterrence against US threat to China's military dominance and security interests in the region. China believes the status quo in East Asian geopolitics serves its strategic interests. Brookings scholar Richard Bush depicts East Asian geopolitics by trying to put himself into China's shoes:

> There is a chain of islands, all of whose governments have security ties with the United States: Japan, Taiwan, and the Philippines. Then there is the southern half of the Korean peninsula, whose government, the Republic of Korea, has a defense treaty with Washington. The only state on China's periphery that does not have close and friendly relations with the United States is North Korea.[34]

Second, China has expressed the concern that North Korean refugees will flood into China if the North's Kim dynasty regime falls. Eleanor Albert, a senior scholar at the Council on Foreign Relations says that China "has helped sustain Kim Jong-un's regime, and has historically opposed harsh international sanctions on North Korea in the hope of avoiding regime collapse and a refugee influx across their 870-mile border."[35] Brookings expert Bush offers the same view:

> The first is a fear that a large number of North Korean citizens, seeking to escape a humanitarian disaster and physical danger would begin coming across the border into China. Indeed, the flow began during the famine of the 1990s and has continued at rather low levels until this day.[36]

The key culprit of the NKNP is of course North Korea itself. However, China has been under international criticism as it has been something of an accomplice of the NKNP. The two reasons mentioned above cannot fully explain the obvious Chinese tolerance, if not active backing, of the NKNP. There are more reasons for the Chinese lack of cooperation for unified international efforts to denuclearize the Korean Peninsula. The Chinese unwillingness to put pressure strong enough to make North Korea abandon its nuclear program will be further elaborated in the next chapter.

Notes:

1 K. Gong, "China's Efforts and the Development of the Six-Party Talks in 2007," CAPS Working Paper Series No. 193 (August 2008), Centre for Asian Pacific Studies (CAPS) of Lingnan University (Hong Kong).

2 J. Bajoria and B. Xu, "The Six Party Talks on North Korea's Nuclear Program," Council on Foreign Relations (2013), https://www.cfr.org/, accessed September 30, 2013.

3 Adapted from the following two sources: "North and South Korea Talks: Timeline of Pyongyang's Nuclear Ambitions," *Telegraph* (2011), https://www.telegraph.

co.uk/, accessed April 21, 2016; "North Korea Profile: Timeline," *BBC* (2018), https://www.bbc.com/news/, accessed June 13, 2018.

4 Ibid.

5 See, for example, E. Revere, "Kim Jong-un Will Not Give Up North Korea's Nuclear Weapons," Brookings Institution (2018), https://www.brookings.edu/, accessed April 9, 2018.

6 See, for example, K. Davenport, "Chronology of U.S.-North Korean Nuclear and Missile Diplomacy," Arms Control Association (2018), https://www.arms-scontrol.org/, accessed November 30, 2018.

7 See, for example, N. Chandran, "The Last Two Times North Korea Said It Was Giving Up Nukes, It Was Lying," *CNBC* (2018), https://www.cnbc.com/, accessed March 9, 2018.

8 For this line of thought, see, for example, North Korea network expert panel, "Should the World Fund Food Aid to North Korea," *Guardian* (2014), https://www.theguardian.com/, accessed September 10, 2014. The article says, "the (international) aid will reinforce the regime by enabling it to purchase military and luxury goods."

9 "North Korea profile: Timeline," *BBC* (2018).

10 See, for example, D. Sanger, "North Koreans Unveil New Plant for Nuclear Use," *New York Times* (2010), https://www.nytimes.com/, accessed November 20, 2010.

11 See, for example, R. Lewis, "North Korea Says It's Tested an ICBM: Here's Why that's a Big Deal," *TIME* (2017), http://time.com/, accessed July 4, 2017.

12 H. Kristensen and R. Norris, "North Korean Nuclear Capabilities, 2018," Vol. 74, Issue 1, *Bulletin of the Atomic Scientists* (2018), https://www.tandfonline.com/, accessed January 8, 2018. "The authors cautiously estimate that North Korea may have produced enough fissile material to build between 30 and 60 nuclear weapons, and that it might possibly have assembled 10 to 20."

13 S. Elegant, "Why the Six-Party North Korea Talks Failed," *TIME* (2006), http://content.time.com/, accessed September 23, 2015.

14 Quoted in A. Tiwathia, "Failure in the Six-Party Talks Was Inevitable," *Foreign Policy* (2006), https://foreignpolicy.com/, accessed December 26, 2006.

15 See, for example, A. Vorontsov, "North Korea's Military-First Policy: A Curse or a Blessing?" Brookings Institution (2006), https://www.brookings.edu/, accessed September 15, 2007.

16 J. Hoare, "*Songun* ('Army First' Policy)," *Historical Dictionary of Democratic People's Republic of Korea* (Lanham, MD: Scarecrow Press, 2012), 352.

17 "Military Doctrine," GlobalSecurity.org (2018), https://www.globalsecurity.org/, accessed September 18, 2018.

18 G. Kim, "The Making of the North Korean State," *Journal of Korean Studies* (Durham, NC: Duke University Press, 2007), Vol. 12, Issue 1 (Fall 2007), 15–42.

19 As for the relationship between *Juche* and *Songun*, see, for example, Z. Beauchamp, "Juche, the State Ideology that Makes North Koreans Revere Kim Jong Un, Explained," *Vox* (2018), https://www.vox.com/, accessed June 18, 2018. Exactly when Kim Il-sung began to develop the *Juche* ideology has yet to come to light.

20 P. French, "North Korea: State of Paranoia," (London: Zed Books, 2014).

21 Korean Overseas Information Service, "Is N.K. Trying an Experiment for Survival?" Korea.net (2002), http://www.korea.net/, accessed April 30, 2007.

22 Concerning the notion that culture is hard to change, see, for example, S. Denning, "How Do You Change an Organizational Culture?" *Forbes* (2011), https://www.forbes.com/, accessed July 23, 2011.

23 See, for example, "Factbox: History of Failure: Efforts to Negotiate on North Korean Disarmament," Reuters (2018), https://www.reuters.com/, accessed March 7, 2018.

24 N. Chandran, "The Last Two Times North Korea Said It Was Giving Up Nukes, It Was Lying."

25 E. Revere, "Kim Jong-un Will Not Give Up North Korea's Nuclear Weapons."

26 Ibid.

27 Hwang offered this view numerous times at South Korean seminars and forums, including those sponsored by Myongji University in Seoul, where he served for a while as an endowed professor.

28 G. Kessler, "History Lesson: China's Reluctance to Pressure North Korea," *Washington Post* (2013), https://www.washingtonpost.com/, accessed April 9, 2013.

29 See, for example, D. Grossman, "China's Reluctance on Sanctions Enforcement in North Korea," RAND Corporation (2018), https://www.rand.org/, accessed January 4, 2018.

30 Concerning Beijing's ambivalence about the sanctions, see, for example, H. Ellyatt, "Stability and Strategy: Why Is China So Easy on North Korea?" *CNBC* (2017), https://www.cnbc.com/, accessed December 6, 2017.

31 See, for example, U. Friedman, "Why China Isn't Doing More to Stop North Korea," *Atlantic* (2017), https://www.theatlantic.com/, accessed August 9, 2017.

32 M. Landler, "Detecting Shift, U.S. Makes Case to China on North Korea," *New York Times* (2013), https://www.nytimes.com/, accessed April 5, 2013.

33 J. Huang, "Here Is What China Wants to See Happen in Asia (and America May Not Like It)," *National Interest* (2017), https://nationalinterest.org/, accessed August 28, 2017.

34 R. Bush, "China's Response to Collapse in North Korea," Brookings Institution (2014), https://www.brookings.edu/, accessed January 23, 2014.

35 E. Albert, "The China–North Korea Relationship," Council on Foreign Relations (2018), https://www.cfr.org/, accessed March 28, 2018.

36 R. Bush, "China's Response to Collapse in North Korea."

CHAPTER 9

CHINA COMPLICATES NORTH KOREAN NUCLEAR ISSUE

From October 14, 2006, to December 22, 2017, the UNSC adopted nine major sanctions resolutions on North Korea in response to the country's nuclear and missile activities. Each resolution condemned North Korea's latest nuclear and ballistic missile activity and called on North Korea to cease its illicit activities, which have violated previous UNSC resolutions.[1] China has been the treacherous actor that has made the six-party talks and the UNSC sanctions against North Korea ineffective.

Beijing has steadily taken a half-hearted approach to North Korean nuclear brinkmanship. For example, following North Korea's sixth nuclear test in September 2017, the UNSC unanimously adopted the strongest yet sanctions against North Korea, which targeted North Korean oil imports, textile exports, and overseas laborers. The sixth nuclear test was also North Korea's most provocative move during Donald Trump's US presidency.[2] However, China offered its backup in advance for what was expected to be a watered-down version of a UNSC resolution. As a result, the US-drafted resolution that initially called for an oil embargo on North Korea, and an asset freeze and travel ban on its leader Kim Jong-un had to be toned down in the hope of securing China's support of the resolution.[3]

The reasons why China has remained so lenient toward North Korea have been touched in part in the preceding chapter. To delve further into the Chinese tolerance of Pyongyang's constant threat to international security reveals Chinese concern about North Korean instability. Dismantling the NKNP would certainly mean a radical change in North Korea whose regime legitimacy is heavily based on the *Songun* policy. Any change in the *Songun* policy would very likely lead to a political instability of an unknown scale in the North. Needless to say, the collapse of the *Songun* policy would decisively unsettle the foundation of the Kim dynasty rule.

China hates to see political instability in North Korea. Brookings scholar Bush attempts to analyze this Chinese concern. He notes that when Beijing has feared instability is growing in North Korea, "it has sought to use its economic, political, and diplomatic influence to reverse that trend."[4] Given the fact that North Korea is China's only military ally in its security parameter in East Asia, China must have every reason to believe that it is in its interest to keep a stable North Korean regime under its influence. For this reason, Chinese leaders consider it as a bad scenario to see a unified Korea under the control of South Korea that will maintain close alliance with the United States, as it is today, but may not be friendly to Beijing. China will hardly support South Korean efforts for a ROK-led reunification of the Korean peninsula as long as South Korea's military alliance with the United States remains strong.[5]

The close China-DPRK relationship is celebrated at the Mass Games in Pyongyang (Source: Creative Commons—CC BY-SA 2.0)

This Chinese stance is ill-advised and myopic, though. China has little reason to be afraid of a US military attack against it unless it destabilizes East Asian security situation for its military hegemony in this region, which is not at all useful to all East Asian actors, including China itself. Given the nature of the world we are living in, which is closely interconnected, a war between the two behemoths would be suicidal to both. Not only United States but also Chinese leaders know enough of this, but knowledge is one thing and practice is another as far as the conventional thought of Chinese leaders is concerned. They are still living in the contemporary world with the nineteenth-century institutions like the one-party communist system and the outdated twentieth-century mind-set. Although Chinese leaders do not fear US military intentions toward them, China still remains suspicious of the US strategic goals in East Asia, contradicting itself. In the minds of most Chinese leaders, the United States is not so much a partner as an adversary.

There are, however, more reasons for China's reluctance to cooperate with the United States to dismantle the NKNP. The NKNP is a critical bargaining chip that China can use against the United States. For the United States, the NKNP is a bone stuck in its throat. On the other hand, Beijing has a lot of pending issues with the United States, including US trade deficit with China as exhibited in the recent US-China trade war, China's alleged currency manipulation, the Taiwan Relations Act, China-US dispute over the South China Sea as demonstrated in the Chinese-built artificial islands in this region with military purposes,[6] terminal high-altitude area defense (THAAD) deployment in South Korea, the US policies toward Tibet, and human rights in China. The tougher the UN sanctions against Pyongyang, the deeper Pyongyang's dependency on Beijing gets. Although China, as North Korea's single lifeline, has the Kim Jong-un regime nearly at its disposal, it has little reason to hurry to pick out North Korea's nuclear bone stuck in US throat when those issues with Washington continue to irk it. Shortly before and after the first Donald Trump–Kim Jong-un summit in June 2018, Chinese leader Xi Jinping and Kim Jong-un had three surprise summits. The third surprise summit between Xi and Kim took place on June 19–20, 2018, just one week after the Trump-Kim summit meeting. When the second Trump-Kim meeting in Vietnam was approaching in early 2019, Xi and Kim had another meeting on January 8, 2019, in Beijing. Considering Xi and Kim didn't meet even once during the first five years they were both in power, Kim's crossing the border into China four times in only ten months of 2018–2019 had special messages for both Xi Jinping and Kim Jong-un to send to the United States.

For Xi Jinping, the first message to Trump was that China has the most powerful leverage over the NKNP. In other words, China was telling the United States that without Beijing's cooperation, the United States could never resolve North Korea's nuclear issue. The second was that China's interest is not consistent with that of United States. China was signaling that it was a key factor for the summit and it would never sit and look on signs of any possible negative impact the meeting could have on its interest.[7] To put it another way, China wanted the international community to recognize that it was an indirect but decisive player in any US–North Korea summit, which could influence the meeting to its own interest. The third was that China would play an aggressive role in any deal between North Korea and the United States. Xi suddenly became more interested in North Korea from 2018 when Kim started making plans to meet South Korean President Moon Jae-in and then Trump. All told, Chinese leader Xi does not want to be left out in any US-DPRK nuclear deal.[8]

For Kim Jong-un, the first message to the United States was that he has a powerful super ally, China. This message became clearer when Kim made a surprise visit to China on January 8, 2019, before the second summit with US president Trump. Zhao Tong of the Carnegie-Tsinghua Center in Beijing told the *Washington Post*:

> Kim Jong Un is not feeling confident about his second summit with Donald Trump, so he is trying to court his Chinese counterpart. This sends a message to the U.S. that, even if the U.S. does not cooperate, even if they keep the economic sanctions, North Korea can still do well with China's support.[9]

In fact, Kim Jong-un already emphasized as much on January 1, 2019, in his New Year's Day speech that apparently pressured the United States:

> If the United States . . . attempts to unilaterally enforce something upon us and persists in imposing sanctions and pressure against our Republic, we may be compelled to find a new way for defending the sovereignty of the country and the supreme interests of the state and for achieving peace and stability of the Korean peninsula.[10]

Kim Jong-un's second message was that he has mentors and strategists, Chinese leaders, notably Xi Jinping, who can teach him how to deal with the United States. In other words, Kim was telling the United States that he would hardly be swung by US hand. When preparations for the second Trump-Kim summit were proceeding in early 2019, Xuan Dongri, director of the Institute of Northeast Asia Studies at Yanbian University in northern China, said to the effect that Kim's surprise visit to Xi on January 8, 2019, could be seen as preparation for the meeting with Trump.[11] The series of Kim's meetings with Xi shortly before and after the Singapore summit were for such preparation. "As a young leader dealing with the United States alone, he needs a country like China to offer advice," Xuan said. "After all, China deals with the United States all the time."[12]

Kim's third message to the United States was that he is interested in searching economic remedies for North Korea. During his short twenty-seven-hour visit to China in early 2019, Kim emphasized industrial growth before heading home. Kim Jong-un made a visit to a famed herbal medicine maker in Beijing on January 9, as he seemingly searched for new avenues for economic development. However, Kim insisted during the fourth trip to China that the North's denuclearization should be gradual and that sanctions should be eased in return for its progress.[13] His insistence could be considered as a message to the United States that Washington's economic assistance, including the lifting of the sanctions, is a precondition for a "gradual" denuclearization of the North.

In sum, the repeated Xi Jinping–Kim Jong-un meetings before and after the first Trump-Kim summit amounted to a warning to Washington from both China and North Korea that a US–North Korea deal could not happen at the cost of the common interest of China and North Korea. It is of course natural in real politics for a nation to typically prioritize national interest over anything else in any international deal.

Although the international community has criticized China's reluctance to do more to stop North Korea's nuclear development program, the Chinese restrained stance toward the NKNP reflects a difference between China's narrowly defined national interest and the general interest of the international community.[14] A reexamination of Chinese attitude toward the NKNP raises a key question. Would the Chinese mildness toward the NKNP really serve its national interest? The answer is certainly "no" for the reasons below.

First, it requires no expert knowledge to say that a large-scale warfare where American troops would march over the so-called buffer zone North Korea to engage the 2.3 million–strong People's Liberation Army of China is simply inconceivable. On top of that, US president Donald Trump has repeated calls for withdrawing American forces from South Korea someday. Trump expressed once again a desire to eventually "bring our soldiers back home" especially after he had the first summit with Kim Jong-un in Singapore.

Trump's successors as US presidents will also determine the issue of stationing US forces in South Korea according to cost-benefit analysis for US national interest. The future of the NKNP will play a key role in the US decision. A North Korean denuclearization is most likely to lead to a pullout, let alone a buildup, of US troops from the Korean Peninsula. It will result in at least a significant reduction of US military presence in the region. For one thing, Seoul and Washington agreed twice—in 2010 and 2014—to delay the US transfer to South Korea of wartime operational control (OPCON) because of Pyongyang's continuing provocations and nuclear and missile threats.[15] Most media reports have supported the view that a denuclearized North Korea would certainly bring about at least a substantial reduction, if not a total withdrawal, of US military presence on the Korean Peninsula. For example, the *Wall Street Journal* reported on May 6, 2018:

> Powerful voices in Washington and Seoul have given a burst of energy to a question long relegated to the margins of public debate: If a peace deal can be struck with Pyongyang, would there be any need for U.S. forces on the Korean Peninsula? The suggestion, once taboo in Washington and Seoul, comes ahead of a planned summit between North Korean leader Kim Jong Un and President Donald Trump.[16]

Nonetheless, the outdated mind-set of Chinese leaders does not embrace the view that the United States has no intention to pose a threat to Chinese security as far as Beijing abides by international norms and practices as a responsible member of the global community. For example, the series of artificial islands China has constructed since 2014 throughout the South China Sea area reflect the Chinese archaic worry about a US military threat.

Despite strong reactions from China's neighbors in the region, including the Philippines, Vietnam, Brunei, and Malaysia, and the unanimous ruling against China of the Permanent Court of Arbitration in The Hague on July 12, 2016, China refused to acknowledge the decision or even the court's jurisdiction. China's island-building efforts require a heavy investment in engineering and infrastructure and could have dire environmental consequences, such as critical damage to coral reefs, which are important to the development of pharmaceuticals, and an extinction of thousands of species in the sea. However, the country is going through all this trouble. China's control of the area may bring some economic benefit to the country, but the true intention of China to control the area is not so much economic as military.[17] On December 13, 2016, the Asian Maritime Transparency Initiative (AMTI) published a report claiming that "China appears to have built significant point-defense capabilities, in the form of large anti-aircraft guns and probable close-in weapons systems (CIWS), at each of its outposts in the Spratly Islands."[18] The report says:

> AMTI began tracking the construction of identical, hexagon-shaped structures at Fiery Cross, Mischief, and Subi Reefs in June and July. It now seems that these structures are an evolution of point-defense fortifications already constructed at China's smaller facilities on Gaven, Hughes, Johnson, and Cuarteron Reefs. China has built nearly identical headquarters buildings at each of its four smaller artificial islands.[19]

The United States has been conducting "freedom of navigation" patrols near the islands and reefs under Chinese control,[20] with the obvious aim to help maintain the stability of the region, which is not against international norms and practices. On the other hand, the Chinese snub of the verdict of the international tribunal at The Hague is against them. The rebuff reflects China's unfounded worry about the country in the region. The AMTI report suggests Beijing's fear of US military operations against it:

> These guns and probable CIWS emplacements show that Beijing is serious about defense of its artificial islands in case of an armed contingency in the South China Sea. Among other things, they would be the last line of defense against cruise missiles launched by the United States or others against these soon-to-be-operational air bases.[21]

After all, the Chinese artificial islands under construction thus remain a gray harbinger of an uncertain future that can undermine the peace and stability of the region as they are likely to unnecessarily infuriate the United States. China does not need to invite troubles that would be to no avail to any party.

Second, speaking of the national interest from economic cooperation between the two countries alone, hundreds of top American companies are operating in China. The Chinese American population numbers some four million. Over 90 percent of Chinese high-tech exports are produced by foreign firms. Washington and Beijing are closely interconnected in many other ways and areas, with global interdependence deepening. Various views have been offered concerning how long the ongoing Sino-America trade war will continue. Whatever their arguments, undeniable is that criticisms of the trade war have been increasing as the fight between the two mega-economies "that lasts 20 years or more is a barely believable idea. It offers an Orwellian vision of ceaseless and debilitating battles between trading blocs—battles that give politicians a convenient enemy and the leverage to impose themselves domestically."[22]

Third, China, whatever its diplomatic rhetoric for a reunification of the Korean Peninsula, prefers the status quo, two Koreas. China hates to see a strong unified Korea arise in its backyard, whether it will remain allied with the United States or not. In this context, it's worth remembering that before West and East Germany were reunified in 1990 in less than a year after the Soviet bloc unraveled, even British prime minister Margaret Thatcher and French president François Mitterrand initially opposed German unification because they feared a more powerful Germany to emerge in Europe.[23] However, Chinese fear of a Korean reunification similar to the German experience is much more acute. China has a unique political culture of hating to see a strong country like Japan emerge in its neighborhood, as it had maintained small vassal or tributary countries in its periphery for thousands of years of its history, according to Lucian W. Pye, the late MIT professor of worldwide fame in Chinese affairs.[24] Pye was born in 1921 in Fenzhou in Shanxi Province in northwest China into a family of congregational missionaries of the American Board of Commissioners for Foreign Missions and grew up in China for nine years of childhood before his family moved to the United States.

However, such psychology of China toward a Korean reunification as a result of a breakdown of the Kim Jong-un regime is not well advised. China, as the world's second largest economy, needs to think outside the box and be able to see the bigger picture for its own interest. If China is concerned about the Sino-American trade dispute, it needs to try to find more markets for its exports in Europe, Asia, Latin America, and so on. A much bigger, more dynamic market economy on the Korean Peninsula that will follow a Korean reunification will serve China's interest much better than now. A strong market economy of a unified Korea would also fundamentally rid the years-old Chinese fear of a refugee exodus from North Korea into its territory. Furthermore, given the geopolitical proximity between China and a unified Korea, close ties between the two sides would be able to provide China with a much stronger and much more constructive deterrence to its perceived US military threat to its interest, as a unified Korea will certainly accommodate America's economic, cultural, and other operations in Korea. In other words, China's engagement of a unified Korea will definitely remove for good the Chinese speculative fear of a US threat to its security interest. If China ever thinks of a reunified Korean Peninsula under its political and military dominance, such an idea would be not only anachronistic but also unrealistic, like pursuing phantoms. China will never be able to dominate over, let alone oppress, the Korean people as it is now doing over Tibetans. If this would ever happen, China would face a strong resistance not only from Koreans but also from the international community, putting in peril the security of East Asia, of which it is a part.

Fourth, China needs to demonstrate toward the international community self-confidence worthy of its reputation as the world's second largest economy and a global superpower. In retrospect, China, contrary to what its name—meaning a flowery country in the center of the world—signifies, had received a cold reception from the international community for a long time, at least since the First Opium War (1839–1842). It was only from 2001, when China could become a member of the World Trade Organization, that Beijing began to draw international recognition as a potential economic power. This history is the main source of Chinese inferiority complex toward the world. Peking University professor Zhang Yiwu succinctly takes note of this Chinese feeling that it is still less important and not a key player in world affairs:

> Though now a bona fide global power, the Chinese
> mentality still struggles with questions of self-con-
> fidence. It's time for the ex "Sick Man of Asia" to
> embody its true strength.[25]

Professor Zhang also says that "Chinese have a centuries-long wolf culture. People's impression of wolves was mainly negative in the past."[26] Many Chinese find wolves scary, which is why there are plentiful stories about wolves harming people and other animals in traditional Chinese culture. Zhang's remark can be interpreted as indicating that the Chinese have somehow had the fear that they are surrounded by wolves across the world.

China, conscious of the international community hoping for a denu-clearized Korean Peninsula, has obviously pretended to do something about the NKNP to improve or at least not to impair its international image. It is a positive development for China's interest that the Chinese have begun seeing "wolves," which have no intention to harm China, in an increasingly positive light, as professor Zhang notes.[27] All told, China's abandonment of its preference of the status quo on the Korean Peninsula over a unified Korea is nearly as important as North Korea's relinquish-ment of nuclear weapons development program. If Xi Jinping leadership decides to play a definitive role in dismantling the NKNP, China's inter-national stature would grow remarkably and Beijing could become a much stronger global leader.

Fortunately for the international community, China has begun to show, at least since late 2017, the signs that it is increasingly getting wor-ried about North Korea's nuclear weapons arsenal. Beijing seems to have realized belatedly that North Korea's WMDs are too dangerous to be left in the hands of a North Korean army caught in political chaos. By now, China may not be opposed even to the idea that the US military does the job of removing North Korea's nuclear weapons, since it does not want nuclear proliferation, especially in its vicinity.[28] In addition, China seems to have realized that it's lukewarm attitude or ambivalence toward the NKNP will only serve to buttress Beijing's identity with Pyongyang, and damage its international reputation to the great disadvantage of China's global interest.

Last but not least, the foundation of China's one-party system seems to be shakier than ever. The economic growth-based authority of the Chinese leadership has now faced a crisis that is more serious than ever before. In this regard, North Korea is obviously a major negative factor for the Chinese economy whose growth rate is decelerating and is foretold to be slowing down for a considerable time to come due in no small part to the trade conflict with the United States. US president Trump has repeatedly suggested that tariffs could be slapped on China if it did not do everything in its power to rein in North Korea.[29] Kim Jong-un is also increasingly becoming a headache to China's domestic politics. On the Chinese Internet, Kim has been mocked as "Kim Fatty the Third" and treated like a badly behaved nephew to Xi Jinping,[30] who is 65, which has become an internal political trouble that Xi Jinping leadership, which is already notorious for human rights oppression, has to address. China's continuing support of North Korea serves to make the authoritarian character of the Xi Jinping regime look analogous to one of the worst tyrannies in the world.

It is too early to predict that China will eventually cooperate with the United States to undo the NKNP in an aggressive manner based on a cool-headed calculation of its national interest. At any rate, the international community will continue to pressure China to play a pivotal role in dismantling the NKNP. All told, despite its current show of alliance with North Korea as a strategic move aiming at the United States, China will have no alternative but embracing the international call for an immediate undoing of the NKNP.

Notes:

1 For the time line of the UN Security Council's sanctions resolutions on North Korea, see, for example, K. Davenport, "UN Security Council

Resolutions on North Korea," Arms Control Association (2018), https://www.armscontrol.org/, accessed January 31, 2018.

2 See, for example, A. Ward, "North Korea Just Tested Its Most Powerful Nuclear Bomb Yet," *Vox* (2017), https://www.vox.com/, accessed September 3, 2017.

3 C. Wong, "China Shows Backing for Watered-Down UN Resolution on North Korea," *South China Morning Post* (2017), https://www.scmp.com/, accessed September 12, 2017.

4 R. Bush, "China's Response to Collapse in North Korea."

5 See, for example, North Korea network expert panel, "China Snubs North Korea with Leader's Visit to South Korea," *Guardian* (2014), https://www.the-guardian.com/, accessed July 3, 2014.

6 See, for example, "China's Maritime Disputes," Council on Foreign Relations (2017), https://www.cfr.org/, accessed January 31, 2017.

7 See, for example, B. Ide, "China Watching Kim-Trump Summit Closely," *Voice of America* (2018), https://www.insidevoa.com/, accessed June 11, 2018.

8 A. Fifield, "Kim Jong Un Shows Trump There are Plenty More—or at Least One More—Fish in the Sea," *Washington Post* (2018), https://www.washington-post.com/, accessed January 8, 2019.

9 Quoted in A. Ward, "Kim Jong Un Made a Surprise Visit to China: It's Mostly about Trump." *Vox* (2019), https://www.vox.com/, accessed January 8, 2019.

10 See, for instance, R. Carlin, "Hints for 2019: Kim Jong Un's New Year's Address," *38 North* (2019), https://www.38north.org/, accessed January 3, 2019.

11 Quoted in A. Fifield, "Kim Jong Un Shows Trump There are Plenty More—or at Least One More—Fish in the Sea."

12 Ibid.

13 O. Nagai, "Kim Tours Beijing Medicine Plant in Search of Economic Remedies," *Nikkei Asian Review* (2019), https://asia.nikkei.com/, accessed January 10, 2019.

14 See, for example, U. Friedman, "Why China Isn't Doing More to Stop North Korea," *Atlantic* (2017), https://www.theatlantic.com/, accessed August 9, 2017.

15 S. Choe, "U.S. and South Korea Agree to Delay Shift in Wartime Command," *New York Times* (2014), https://www.nytimes.com/, accessed October 25, 2014.

16 J. Cheng and A. Jeong, "U.S. Troops in South Korea Emerge as Potential Bargaining Chip," *Wall Street Journal* (2018), https://www.wsj.com/, accessed May 6, 2018.

17 W. Nicol, "Showdown in the South China Sea: China's Artificial Islands Explained," *Digital Trends* (2017), https://www.digitaltrends.com/, accessed May 3, 2017.

18 AMTI, "China's New Spratly Island Defenses," Asian Maritime Transparency Initiative (AMTI) (2016), https://amti.csis.org/, accessed December 30, 2016.

19 Ibid.

20 W. Nicol, "Showdown in the South China Sea: China's Artificial Islands Explained."

21 AMTI, "China's New Spratly Island Defenses."

22 "A Long Trade War Will Leave the World Feeling Its Piggy Bank Was Robbed," *Guardian* (2018), https://www.theguardian.com/, accessed September 23, 2018.

23 J. Goldgeier, "What North and South Korea Can Learn from German Reunification," *Washington Post* (2018), https://www.washingtonpost.com/, accessed April 28, 2018.

24 L. Pye, *The Spirit of Chinese Politics*, new edition (Cambridge, MA: Harvard University Press, 1992).

25 Y. Chang, "China Still Fighting Its Own Inferiority Complex," *World Crunch* (2015), https://www.worldcrunch.com/, accessed August 9, 2015.

26 Quoted in X. Wei and J. Huang, "New Documentary about Orphaned Wolf Cub Dispels Misunderstandings about Wolves," *Global Times* (2017), http://www.globaltimes.cn/, accessed June 22, 2017.

27 Ibid.

28 See, for example, Q. Jia, "It Is Time for China to Prepare for the Worst in North Korea," *National Interest* (2017), https://nationalinterest.org/, accessed September 12, 2017.

29 See, for example, A. Fifield, "Kim Jong Un Shows Trump There are Plenty More—or at Least One More—Fish in the Sea."

30 Ibid.

Chapter 10

NORTH KOREA WILL NEVER ABANDON NUCLEAR WEAPONS

US president Donald Trump said on June 21, 2018, that North Korea had already begun to denuclearize, trumpeting the results of his first meeting in Singapore with the North Korean leader Kim Jong-un. International society hoped the second Trump-Kim summit held in Hanoi, Vietnam, on February 27–28, 2019, could make a more substantial, concrete progress toward North Korea's denuclearization than the first summit. However, the second summit ended in a failure.

Kim Jong-un is well known for his erratic behavior. The developments in US–North Korea relations during even less than a month after the first summit had shown the unpredictable pattern of Kim's behavior with respect to the protracted issue of North Korea's denuclearization. Will Kim Jong-un really begin the denuding? Will North Korea dump its nuclear weapons altogether in a short period? In Hanoi, Kim Jong-un said he wouldn't be holding a second summit with US president Trump if he weren't willing to make good on his denuclearization pledge. However, analysts remained as suspicious of Kim's intentions as ever after the Hanoi summit. Their distrust of Kim is based on the reasons below.

First, North Korea has already become one of the nuclear-armed states of the world. Nuclear powers are generally categorized into four groups.[1] The states in the first group are called NPT-designated nuclear weapon states. This group has five states—China, France, Russia, United Kingdom, and United States. The second group called non-NPT nuclear powers has three states—North Korea, India, and Pakistan. The third group called North Atlantic Treaty Organization (NATO) member nuclear weapons sharing states has five states—Belgium, Germany, Italy, the Netherlands, and Turkey. Israel in the fourth group is suspected to have nuclear weapons. To add another category, the fifth, Iran has a very contentious nuclear program, with the future of the so-called Iran deal remaining uncertain. To be eligible to be a nuclear weapon state as categorized above, North Korea has used so many tricks and made so much effort as mentioned so far that it would be naïve for any well-advised analyst to conclude North Korea will ditch nuclear weapons as easily as the international community wishes.

Second, for the North Korean regime, nuclear weapons are the foremost symbol of national power, pride, and prestige as well as the most practical tool to threaten the international community and to oppress its own people. However, in this age in which incredible advances in technology are constantly being made, nuclear weapons have no technological value. To remove them from North Korea according to a North Korean consent would also be too costly for any country, except for the United States, to be willing to perform the job.[2] Nevertheless, nuclear weapons are so destructive that it is attractive to a destitute, adventurous country like North Korea that wants to punch above its weight toward international society.[3] In short, nuclear weapons are too precious in North Korean eyes to be traded away for any rewards to be achieved after denuclearization.[4] The young Kim Jong-un who assumed office as supreme leader of North Korea in 2011 at the age of twenty-seven—Kim was born January 8, 1984, according to American records—must be believing that to surrender nuclear weapons that he believes would protect his security and elevate his international power and influence will precipitate the end of his iron grip on his country that may otherwise outlive almost forty-eight years of dictatorship of his grandfather Kim Il-sung—the second longest despotism in the world since 1900 that follows more than fifty-two years of absolute rule of Fidel Castro of Cuba.

North Korea demands the elimination of the hostile policy of the United States toward North Korea and a US security guarantee for the Kim Jong-un regime as a precondition for its denuclearization. Washington is indeed willing to offer North Korea a security guarantee if it embarks on such denuclearization. However, Kim Jong-un knows his regime cannot remain safe permanently under a US security guarantee. Kim must be remembering that Libyan leader Muammar Gaddafi could not survive the Libyan Civil War in which US-led NATO supported the insurrection against Gaddafi's despotism. To elaborate, Kim Jong-un knows well how miserable the last moment of Gaddafi was. "In a surprise move in 2003, Gaddafi agreed to give up his nuclear weapons program and welcome international inspectors. In exchange, the U.S. and its allies promised better relations with Libya and lifted long-standing economic sanctions."[5] Eight years later, however, NATO invaded Libya, ending the forty-two-year tyranny of Gaddafi.[6] The rebels shot Gaddafi to death as he pleaded for his life by offering gold and money. It is certain that Kim keeps Gaddafi's tragic end in mind, and it deters him and his subordinates within the North Korean leadership from surrendering their own nuclear weapons.[7] Remembering Gaddafi's last moment, Kim must have thought it would be extremely dangerous for him to concede to American demand for abandoning his nuclear weapons. In other words, Kim believes that that any external security guarantee cannot better ensure his regime security than his own nuclear weapons. Kim's demand for a US security guarantee reflects his intention to sidetrack the core issue of US–North Korea talks—a North Korean denuclearization.

Third, there is a conceptual gap. In the wake of the first Trump-Kim summit in particular, it looked as if a denuclearized North Korea might emerge as a reality in the near future. However, there is a drastic conceptual difference in "denuclearization" between North Korean thought and that of the international community. The United States, South Korea, Japan, and the rest of international society have an identical concept about a dismantlement of the NKNP, but it is widely different from that of North Korea. For one thing, as Bookings scholar Evans Revere notes, North Korea's concept of "denuclearization" is in no way a genuine denuclearization and "bears no resemblance to the American definition." Revere writes:

> Those who have negotiated nuclear matters with Pyongyang know that Kim's words were a familiar North Korean demand to end the "threat" posed by the U.S.–South Korea alliance, the presence of U.S. troops in Korea, and the nuclear umbrella that defends South Korea and Japan.[8]

Revere notes that North Korea's concept of "denuclearization" amounts to "arms control," meaning North Korean status as a nuclear weapon state already stands firm as a rock today. Revere's notion is essentially the same as that of another Brookings scholar, Ivo H. Daalder, about North Korea's no more testing, a freeze on plutonium production, the return of international monitors, and so on as mentioned above. Revere takes note of how it would be difficult to denuclearize North Korea, if it could ever happen:

> A senior North Korean official once explained to a group of American experts, "If you remove those (US, South Korean and Japanese) threats, we will feel more secure and in ten to twenty years' time we may be able to consider denuclearization. In the mean-time," he continued, "we are prepared to meet with you as one nuclear weapon state with another to discuss arms control."[9]

US Naval War College professor James Holmes offers a generalization about the near impossibility of denuclearizing an existing nuclear-armed state. "Nuclear powers seldom relinquish their arms. Nor should we expect them to. That insight should guide U.S. strategy going forward."[10]

Fourth, there is the issue of applying double standards. In this context, a simple question that relates to the three non-NPT nuclear states—India,

North Korea, and Pakistan—can be raised. The three nuclear powers are different from one another in military and political aspects and the reasons to have nuclear weapons. Even so, our common sense should prepare for a North Korean reaction, "Don't apply double standards to us." The fact that North Korea is one of the six rogue states—North Korea, Iran, Sudan, Cuba, Syria, and Venezuela—and is one of four states—Iran, North Korea, Sudan, and Syria—that are on the list of "State Sponsors of Terrorism" would not be enough for the international community to apply double standards to North Korea, especially given the fact that many analysts have argued that Pakistan and India pose more serious nuclear threat to international security than North Korea.[11] The international community is worried that the NKNP would enable Pyongyang to sell nuclear materials and nuclear weapons data to other nations or terrorist groups.[12] North Korea would argue, however, that there has been no proven record of selling nuclear materials or data to other countries or terrorist groups. It would also claim that there is no fact-based conclusion that precludes the possibility for Pakistan and India to sell such things to rogue states and terrorists under any circumstances. In fact, Pakistan has been able to avoid being added to the list of rogue states because the United States had long maintained close relations with Islamabad—a vestige of the Cold War.[13]

Fifth, it is impossible to destroy the knowledge—which is not physical—about nuclear weapons that North Korea has already accumulated. This knowledge has already become a part of North Korean body of knowledge about nuclear science and engineering and would permit North Korea to carry out further research in secret and resume a nuclear weapons program at short notice at any time. Generally speaking, knowledge and experience once earned has the innate trait to continuously increase rather than decrease. Before the first Trump-Kim summit, the United States told North Korea that it must destroy all its nuclear weapons data and send an estimated ten thousand nuclear scientists currently in North Korea—including two hundred core leaders, two thousand experts, and six thousand technicians—abroad, as well as start shipping nuclear weapons, fissile material, and some of its long-range missiles out of the country within a couple of months of the summit. However, the North Korean regime refused the US requests.[14]

In a sense, North Korea cannot but refuse to comply with the US demand. As human beings, nuclear scientists anywhere in the world should be allowed at least the freedom to choose the country where they want to reside. North Korean leader Kim Jong-un, however despotic, could not forcibly "export" the ten thousand nuclear scientists abroad against their will. Is the United States going to bring them to Oak Ridge, Tennessee? This is an entirely unrealistic call. The Oak Ridge National Laboratory is a nuclear research and storage facility that holds key components from Libya's nuclear weapons program.[15] Should they be locked up behind the bars in a hypothetical camp within or near the Oak Ridge facility or somewhere else? Should they be put under house arrest?

As history provides us food for thought, we need to remember Operation Overcast that was later renamed Operation Paperclip—a secret program of the US Joint Intelligence Objectives Agency (JIOA) largely carried out by special agents of the US Army Counter Intelligence Corps (CIC)—in which more than one thousand six hundred German scientists, engineers, and technicians (along with their families) were brought to the United States to work on America's behalf during the Cold War. They were taken to the United States for government employment, primarily between 1945 and 1959, but not against their will.[16] The secret plan to bring Nazi scientists,[17] including Nobel laureates, to the United States began even earlier. Before the birth of the Manhattan Project in 1939, the United States was secretly competing with Nazi Germany to be the first to develop atomic bombs. Atomic Heritage Foundation writes:

> The United States government became aware of the German nuclear program in August 1939, when Albert Einstein wrote to President Roosevelt, warning "that it may become possible to set up a nuclear chain reaction in a large mass of uranium by which vast amounts of power and large quantities of new radium-like elements would be generated." The United States was in

a race to develop an atomic bomb believing whoever
had the bomb first would win the war.[18]

In the 1930s and the 1940s, making nuclear weapons was considered high-est-level rocket science. Not only the United States but also the Soviet Union was aggressive in forcibly recruiting—even at gunpoint in the case of the Soviet Union—nuclear scientists and engineers who had been put to work for the Third Reich of Germany.[19] Nowadays, numerous countries on earth can make atomic bombs if they choose to and if it had not been for international sanctions. Who would like to accommodate the nuclear specialists from North Korea? In a nuclear-free North Korea and outside of it, North Korean nuclear specialists could find new jobs. Theoretically, the United States could, for example, enable North Korean nuclear specialists to work for labs specializing in the peaceful use of atomic energy if they want to.

The Kim Jong-un regime, for its part, has a more critical reason to reject the US demand that North Korea's nuclear personnel be sent abroad. We need to remember at this point that North Korea was formed as a "Big Lie" state. The "Big Lie" had spawned the personality cult surrounding the North Korean Kim dynasty referred to as the Mount Paektu Bloodline. The US demand for North Korean denuclearization presupposes North Korea's opening up to the international community. If North Korea ever opened up to the global community, the personality cult surrounding the Kim dynasty would be unveiled as a "Big Lie" not only to the global community but also to the North Korean people. If this were to happen, the legitimacy of the Kim dynasty regime would certainly crumble, and its existence would then be endangered. Kim Jong-un is most afraid of this prospect. As a result, it is most certainly the least of probabilities for North Korea to open up to international society. Since North Korea has to continue to remain isolated from the rest of the world for this reason, it cannot but continue to remain weak and vulnerable vis-à-vis the international community, especially the United States that North Korea has been most fearful of. Under the circumstances, Kim Jong-un believes developing nuclear weapons and other WMDs to provoke the international community, to maintain tension with it, and to create fear among his populace is the only way to ensure his security.

The bottom line is that without Kim Jong-un's genuine commitment to denuclearization, North Korea could never be completely denuclearized. In retrospect, major talks between Washington and Pyongyang for North Korean denuclearization started in 1985 when North Korea reluctantly acceded to the NPT, leaving an IAEA safeguards agreement incomplete. For the last three and a half decades since, all talks between the two countries were "the culmination of months, even years, of diplomatic spadework by successive administrations."[20] The two Trump-Kim meetings in 2018–2019 followed decades of failed US talks with the most reclusive, bizarre, anachronistic kingdom on the earth. Why was the first summit in the history of the two countries' relations possible? The answer requires no sophisticated knowledge. Analysts agree that it was possible because Pyongyang's nuclear weapons and missile programs are far more advanced now than in any previous time. In other words, North Korea could enter any talks "in a new position of strength," as Jenny Town of Johns Hopkins University's US-Korea Institute notes.[21] To put it more simply, North Korea is already one of the three non-NPT nuclear-armed states as noted. It is now talking and will talk with any nation, be it the United States, South Korea, or Japan, in the capacity of an official nuclear state or from a status with such capacity. The Trump-Kim summit in Singapore signified the zenith of an international heralding of North Korea as a full-fledged nuclear-armed state.

To put it another way, Kim Jong-un came to Vietnam to strengthen his international status as leader of a nuclear-armed state that was once validated in Singapore. Contrary to Kim Jong-un's remark that he wouldn't come to Vietnam "if he weren't willing to make good on his denuclearization pledge,"[22] Kim came to Hanoi to seek a US easing of economic sanctions against North Korea, not to abandon his nuclear arsenal. It was no wonder that the second Trump-Kim summit in Vietnam failed to reach an agreement.

In fact, the breakdown in the second Trump-Kim talks in Hanoi was anticipated well enough when the first summit talks seemed to have ended in a trumpet blast with no substance. Shortly after the Singapore summit, analysts already began to note, based on new satellite images that indicate Pyongyang is pushing ahead with weapons programs even as it pursues dialogue with Washington. They contend that North Korea has been upgrading nuclear arsenal and missile-manufacturing sites, despite its public pledge to denuclearize during the Singapore summit with US president Donald Trump.[23] Only about two months after the first summit, North Korea was found pressing ahead with nuclear and missile programs. According to a report by the *Guardian*:

> The evidence obtained this month is the latest to suggest ongoing activity at North Korea's nuclear and missile facilities despite talks with the US and a June summit between North Korean leader, Kim Jong-un, and Donald Trump. Mintaro Oba, a former US diplomat who worked on North Korea policy, said: "It reflects an important fact: despite what US officials have been saying, North Korea didn't commit to much of anything on denuclearization."[24]

On October 7, 2018, US secretary of state Mike Pompeo met with Kim Jong Un in Pyongyang. US–North Korea talks per se, whether they are between Trump and Kim or Pompeo and Kim or between any others representing the two sides, may be considered urgent, especially after US president Trump once enabled, in the Singapore summit, North Korean leader Kim Jong-un to gain legitimacy as a nuclear power, something that Pyongyang has gone after persistently. Shortly after the meeting with Kim, Pompeo said that he left North Korea with at least one "major" concession from Kim Jong-un on denuclearization: The North Korean dictator agreed to allow international inspectors in to see the country's Punggye-ri nuclear test site.[25]

The statement by Pompeo was debatable, though. Kim's agreement with the international inspection of the nuclear test site in northeastern North Korea had raised questions rather than given answers as to a North Korean denuclearization. When the three tunnels were demolished at the

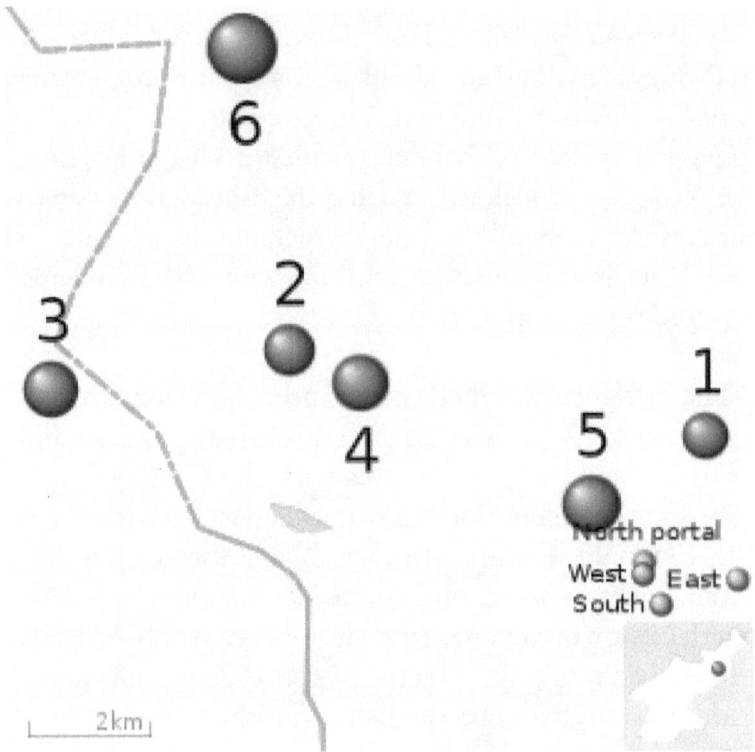

Locations of North Korea's Nuclear Tests: 1: 2006; 2: 2009; 3: 2013; 4: 2016-01; 5: 2016-09; 6: 2017 (Source: The United States Geological Survey)

site in Punggye-ri on May 24, 2018, only about three weeks before the first US–North Korea summit, North Korea invited a select group of foreign journalists only to "watch" the destruction. No experts from the UN or any other independent body were allowed to be present to verify whether the site had been completely destroyed, or whether it could be repaired should North Korea decide to resume testing.[26] Analysts suspected that the demolition of the test site in Punggye-ri prior to the Trump-Kim meeting was a mere diplomatic gesture of rapprochement with the United States that lacked substance. The *Atlantic* reported:

> Goodwill gestures at the outset of negotiations, when there's little trust among the parties, tend to

be provisional. Experts suspect, for instance, that the North Koreans may still be able to reopen the nuclear-test site that they claimed to have destroyed with great fanfare in the lead-up to the summit.[27]

Although there was no evidence that the North Koreans had entirely blown up "four of their big test sites," whether nuclear or missile-related,[28] Kim Jong-un could try to "sell" the demolition of the Punggye-ri site at least twice for two goals as follows. First, Kim let foreign reporters in on the site demolition to show his pretentious willingness to denuclearize North Korea with the aim to make his summit with Trump happen. Kim Jong-un must have been greatly shocked when Trump once canceled his "long-planned meeting" with Kim "based on the tremendous anger and open hostility displayed in Kim Jong-un's most recent statement,"[29] just a few hours after Kim made a show of dismantling the nuclear test site. Second, Kim Jong-un tried to "sell" the test site demolition when he showed Pompeo his intention to allow international inspectors in. Kim's concession to Pompeo for international inspection of the nuclear test site was believed to reflect his apparent effort to gain economic and other benefits from the United States, such as lifting or loosening US economic sanctions on North Korea. Even with his expressed intent to allow international evaluators in, it remained uncertain how the details of the checkup would be carried out. In fact, already on November 3, 2018, North Korea "warned it could revive a state policy aimed at strengthening its nuclear arsenal if the United States does not lift economic sanctions against the country."[30]

In addition, the test site demolition has another significant advantage for not only North Korea but also China. The assumption that North Korea's nuclear weapons may play an important role as a deterrence for China against US military presence in East Asia is one thing, and North Korea's nuclear tests in China's backyard is quite another. In other words, China may not be against North Korea's nuclear weapons program, but objects to the threat of radioactive contamination from the Punggye-ri site blanketing the Chinese living near the site. For instance, Chinese residents

THE WHITE HOUSE
WASHINGTON
May 24, 2018

His Excellency
Kim Jong Un
Chairman of the State Affairs Commission
 of the Democratic People's Republic of Korea
Pyongyang

Dear Mr. Chairman:

We greatly appreciate your time, patience, and effort with respect to our recent negotiations and discussions relative to a summit long sought by both parties, which was scheduled to take place on June 12 in Singapore. We were informed that the meeting was requested by North Korea, but that to us is totally irrelevant. I was very much looking forward to being there with you. Sadly, based on the tremendous anger and open hostility displayed in your most recent statement, I feel it is inappropriate, at this time, to have this long-planned meeting. Therefore, please let this letter serve to represent that the Singapore summit, for the good of both parties, but to the detriment of the world, will not take place. You talk about your nuclear capabilities, but ours are so massive and powerful that I pray to God they will never have to be used.

I felt a wonderful dialogue was building up between you and me, and ultimately, it is only that dialogue that matters. Some day, I look very much forward to meeting you. In the meantime, I want to thank you for the release of the hostages who are now home with their families. That was a beautiful gesture and was very much appreciated.

If you change your mind having to do with this most important summit, please do not hesitate to call me or write. The world, and North Korea in particular, has lost a great opportunity for lasting peace and great prosperity and wealth. This missed opportunity is a truly sad moment in history.

Sincerely yours,

Donald J. Trump
President of the United States of America

An official letter from President Donald Trump to Kim Jong-un
(Source: White House release on May 24, 2018)

of Jilin province, about sixty miles from Punggye-ri, have expressed safety fears and Jilin authorities had to shutter a scenic tourist spot near the North Korean border.[31]

Chinese president Xi Jinping needs to take effective steps to protect Chinese citizens from the North's nuclear fallout. A continuing tolerance or disregard by the Chinese government of the North's nuclear tests near the Chinese border could turn out to be a serious challenge to Xi Jinping government's stability. As far as China remains North Korea's lifeline and only significant ally, Pyongyang has every reason to be wary of the Chinese citizens' reaction to its nuclear tests. North Korea needed to demolish the Punggye-ri site and to build a new nuclear site away from the Chinese border, which would replace the Punggye-ri site, even if it is fixable. According to a study by Chinese geologists, the Punggye-ri test site had collapsed under the stress of multiple explosions, rendering it unsafe for further testing and leaving it vulnerable to radiation leaks.[32]

In more detail, the Punggye-ri site had to be demolished anyway, although two other tunnels in the site were still considered capable of supporting future tests. The dismantlement of the site could meet two North Korean necessities—to alleviate the Chinese fear and to continue to advance its nuclear program in new facilities it wishes to erect—ironically, with US economic help. To recap, North Korea needs money to rebuild a nuclear complex away from the Chinese border. Nuclear scientist Siegfried Hecker observes that "North Korea could surely excavate and prepare new tunnels."[33] It is admitted that, as Hecker indicates, it must be a considerable challenge to North Korea to start over or complete an existing tunnel complex for testing as it will cost much time and money.[34] Consequently, North Korea is already demanding and will continue to demand that Washington lift economic sanctions against it in the series of nuclear talks with Washington, especially after the Singapore summit. North Korea has improved its ability to construct and manage nuclear test sites safely.

The second Trump-Kim summit in Vietnam collapsed since Kim Jong-un tried to cheat the United States again. "Kim was willing to close some but not all nuclear sites in North Korea in exchange for the lifting of all international sanctions."[35] The breakdown of the summit talks in Hanoi amounts to a US warning to Kim Jong-un that if the North Korean leader is shouting "Wolf! Wolf!" for the third time, like the shepherd boy in an Aesop fable, he will face a disaster.

In sum, Kim Jong-un has tried to trade something that has little real value with great benefit. Destroying the nuclear weapons test site and dismantling a missile test facility were low-to-no-cost moves for Pyongyang, given the advanced state of the North's nuclear and missile programs.[36] The successful dismantlement of the Punggye-ri test site indicated a suitable geologic site, meticulous tunnel design and construction, and strong containment practices.[37] Critics have supported the notion of Kim Jong-un's attempt to sell the good-for-nothing nuclear complex at Punggye-ri for a good price:

> North Korea's destruction of the Punggye-ri nuclear test site, even if verified, is not as significant as it might seem. "They don't need the facility to test. They did the testing. They've got the weapon," former Secretary of State John Kerry said at a foreign policy forum in Washington on Friday. "Now they're just building up the arsenal," Kerry said, adding that the U.S. doesn't know where North Korea is hiding its weapons cache.[38]

Overall, as the suspicion surrounding Kim Jong-un's underlying motive behind his ambiguous commitment in Singapore to "working toward" denuclearization of North Korea has become increasingly prevalent, there has been little diplomatic progress of substance until early 2019, about nine months after the Trump-Kim summit. With signs mounting of a deadlock over how to achieve the goal of the denuclearization, US president Trump said on November 7, 2018, the United States was "in no rush" after talks between his top diplomat Mike Pompeo and senior North Korean envoy Kim Yong-chol were postponed, throwing stalled diplomacy over the North's nuclear weapons into further uncertainty.[39] The United States and North Korea had kept talking about another round of Trump-Kim summit until the end of 2018.

As the second Trump-Kim summit eventually happened in Vietnam, a country that represents a successful case of economic reforms, and broke down abruptly with no deal, the uncertainty of the future of a North Korean denuclearization increased. The failed Vietnam summit clearly proved that the leaders of the two countries came there with very different goals. US president Trump wishes North Korea to follow the Vietnamese model of economic success. On the other hand, Kim Jong-un intends to make North Korea a nuclear-armed Vietnam. Kim also sought a US relaxing of economic sanctions against North Korea during the summit. Undeniable is that there will continue to be a big difference between Washington and Pyongyang over the issue of a North Korean denuclearization in the days ahead. Only two days after the meeting in Vietnam between United States and North Korean leaders broke down without them reaching a deal on denuclearization, new satellite images suggested North Korea was restoring the Sohae Satellite Launching Station it had pledged to dismantle.[40] The North Korean move suggested that the Kim Jong-un regime has little intention to denuclearize North Korea and is seeking US concessions, while taking provocative actions against the international community.

At this point, it seems appropriate to put together the three things that the Kim Jong-un regime would never ditch—the personality cult surrounding the ruling Kim family of the Mount Paektu Bloodline, absolute despotism and the *Songun* policy whose core is the six-decade-long nuclear development program.

Notes:

1 See, for example, "Nuclear Weapons: Who Has What at a Glance," Arms Control Association (2018), https://www.armscontrol.org/, accessed June 21, 2018.

2 Q. Jia, "It Is Time for China to Prepare for the Worst in North Korea."

3 G. Friedman, "3 Maps That Explain the Geopolitics of Nuclear Weapons," Mauldin Economics (2017), http://www.mauldineconomics.com/, accessed April 21, 2017.

4 L. Cui, "Why It's Nearly Impossible to Denuclearize North Korea," *Diplomat* (2018), https://thediplomat.com/, June 22, 2018.

5 S. Yuen, "How the Miserable Death of Moammar Gaddafi Factors into Kim Jong Un's Nuclear Ambitions," *CNBC* (2017), https://www.cnbc.com/, accessed July 31, 2017.

6 A. Madambashi, "Gaddafi Dead: Dictator Begged for His Life before Being Killed," *Christian Post* (2011) https://www.christianpost.com/, accessed October 22, 2011.

7 S. Yuen, "How the Miserable Death of Moammar Gaddafi Factors into Kim Jong Un's Nuclear Ambitions."

8 E. Revere, "Kim Jong-un Will Not Give Up North Korea's Nuclear Weapons," Brookings Institution (2018), https://www.brookings.edu/, accessed April 9, 2018.

9 Ibid.

10 J. Holmes, "History Tells Us North Korea Will Never Give Up Its Nuclear Weapons," *National Interest* (2018), https://nationalinterest.org/, accessed June 1, 2018.

11 See, for example, D. DePetris, "Forget North Korea: Pakistan Might Be the Real Nuclear Threat," *National Interest* (2018), https://nationalinterest.org/, accessed August 2, 2018; K. Mizokami, "Forget North Korea: This Is the Most Likely Place a Nuclear War Could Break Out," *National Interest* (2017), https://nation-alinterest.org/, accessed May 19, 2017.

12 J. Ryall and N. Smith, "US Pressures North Korea to Ship Nuclear Weapons Overseas before Sanctions Lifted, according to Reports," *Telegraph* (2018), https://www.telegraph.co.uk/, accessed May 14, 2018.

13 R. Melanson, "Post–Cold War Policy—Isolating and Punishing 'Rogue' States," *Encyclopedia of the New American Nation* (2016), http://www.americanforeignrelations.com/, accessed December 30, 2016.

14 J. Ryall and N. Smith, "US Pressures North Korea to Ship Nuclear Weapons Overseas before Sanctions Lifted, according to Reports."

15 Ibid.

16 A. Jacobsen, *Operation Paperclip: The Secret Intelligence Program to Bring Nazi Scientists to America.* (New York: Little, Brown, 2014). Prologue.

17 For the secret plan, see also, M. Callahan, "Behind the Secret Plan to Bring Nazi Scientists to US," *New York Post* (2014), https://nypost.com/, accessed February 1, 2014.

18 "German Atomic Bomb Project," Atomic Heritage Foundation (2016), https://www.atomicheritage.org/, accessed October 18, 2016.

19 See, for example, L. Schumm, "What was Operation Paperclip?" *HISTORY* (2014), https://www.history.com/, accessed June 2, 2014.

20 R. Gramer and E. Tamkin, "Decades of U.S. Diplomacy with North Korea: A Timeline," *Foreign Policy* (2018), https://fpgroup.foreignpolicy.com/, accessed March 12, 2018.

21 Quoted in R. Gramer and E. Tamkin, "Decades of U.S. Diplomacy with North Korea: A Timeline."

22 "N. Korean Leader Says He's Willing to Denuclearize," Associated Press (2019), https://www.vindy.com/, accessed February 28, 2019.

23 See, for example, J. Cheng, "North Korea Expands Key Missile-Manufacturing Plant," *Wall Street Journal* (2018), https://www.wsj.com/, accessed July 1, 2018.

24 B. Haas, "North Korea: US 'Detects New Activity' at ICBM Factory," *Guardian* (2018), https://www.theguardian.com/, accessed August 14, 2018.

25 D. Shesgreen and T. Maresca, "Secretary of State Mike Pompeo Touts Progress, with Few Details, after Kim Jong Un Meeting," *USA Today* (2018), https://www.usatoday.com/, accessed October 8, 2018.

26 S. Choe, "North Korea's Big Moment Is Upended by Trump," *New York Times* (2018), https://www.nytimes.com/, accessed May 24, 2018.

27 U. Friedman, "Here's What Trump Actually Achieved with North Korea," *Atlantic* (2018), https://www.theatlantic.com/, accessed June 19, 2018.

28 S. Choe, "Fact Check: Is There Truth to Trump's Bold Claims About North Korean Denuclearization?" *New York Times* (2018), https://www.nytimes.com/, accessed June 22, 2018.

29 An official letter from president Donald Trump to Kim Jong-un, a White House release on May 24, 2018.

30 T. Kim, "North Korea Warns that It Will Revive Nuclear Program if U.S. Does Not Lift Sanctions," *TIME* (2018), http://time.com/, accessed November 3, 2018.

31 See, for example, S. Hecker, "Why Did Kim Jong Un Blow up His Nuclear Test Site?" *Washington Post* (2018), https://www.washingtonpost.com/, accessed May 30, 2018.

32 J. McCurry, "North Korea Nuclear Test Site Has Collapsed and May Be Out of Action: China Study," *Guardian* (2018), https://www.theguardian.com/, accessed April 26, 2018.

33 S. Hecker, "Why did Kim Jong Un Blow up His Nuclear Test Site?"

34 Ibid.

35 Live Briefing of *New York Times*, "Trump-Kim Summit Updates: 'Sometimes You Have to Walk,' Trump Says as Talks Collapse," *New York Times* (2019), https://www.nytimes.com/, accessed February 28, 2019.

36 E. Brewer and J. Pak, "How to Tell When North Korea Starts to Denuclearize," *Atlantic* (2018), https://www.theatlantic.com/, accessed October 10, 2018.

37 S. Hecker, "Why Did Kim Jong Un Blow up His Nuclear Test Site?"

38 D. Shesgreen and T. Maresca, "Secretary of State Mike Pompeo Touts Progress, with Few Details, after Kim Jong Un Meeting."

39 M. Pennington, "Trump Says He's 'in No Rush' after N. Korea Talks Postponed," *Stars and Stripes* (2018), https://www.stripes.com/, accessed November 7, 2018.

40 See, for example, "North Korea Rebuilding Sohae Rocket Launch Site, Say Observers," *BBC* (2019), https://www.bbc.com/, accessed March 6, 2019.

CHAPTER 11

PRESIDENT TRUMP EARNS NOTHING
FROM THE TWO SUMMITS

When the second summit between US president Trump and North Korean leader Kim ended in failure on February 28, 2019, Trump said at a press conference in Hanoi:

> It was about the sanctions basically. They wanted the sanctions lifted in their entirety and we couldn't do that . . . Sometimes you have to walk, and this was just one of those times. There is a gap. We have to have sanctions. There is a gap. We have to have sanctions and he wants to denuke. But he wants to just do areas that are less important than the areas that we want.[1]

In short, North Korea wanted a lifting of US economic sanctions in return for partial denuclearization, which amounts to no denuclearization. In denuking a country, there cannot be any such thing as "partial" denuclearization, which is absolutely a misnomer. In detail, North Korea offered to the United States a dismantlement of the nuclear complex at Yongbyon, but the United States knows North Korea has other nuclear facilities, including the Kangson uranium enrichment site and other covert nuclear facilities, which are more important to the North's nuclear activities today than the Yongbyon nuclear facility. The North Korean offer was nothing but another attempt by Kim Jong-un to cheat the United States.

The failed Hanoi summit reminded the international community of a few goodwill moves Kim Jong-un had taken toward the United States after the Singapore summit, such as the return of the remains of American soldiers killed during the Korean War, which had little to do with the central issue of dismantling the NKNP. Trump walked away from the first summit with Kim with a Joint Declaration whose gist—denuclearizing the Korean Peninsula—was practically absent. Consequently, most analysts have played down the meaning of the first Trump-Kim encounter. The *Washington Post* characterized the Trump-Kim meeting as "a summit without substance." The *Post* said:

> The Singapore summit was a mesmerizing spectacle utterly lacking in substance. In other words, it was a perfect microcosm of the Trump presidency . . . Kim won an invaluable propaganda windfall: Ruling one of the poorest (North Korea's gross domestic product is smaller than Vermont's) and most despotic countries in the world, he was recognized as an equal by the leader of the world's sole superpower—not just an equal, indeed, but a valued friend.[2]

"North Korea had given no reliable indication that it was willing to give up its weapons unilaterally as the Trump administration demanded."[3] The phrase, "to work toward denuclearization of the Korean Peninsula" in particular had yet to be clarified. Apart from the issue of whether Kim Jong-un is serious about denuclearization, North Korea regime's definition of denuclearization has been for many years that of the "Korean Peninsula at large," referring to the US nuclear umbrella over South Korea and Japan and the removal of US troop presence.[4]

The first summit was just the resumption of the US–North Korean negotiations that have produced no results for denuclearization for some forty years, only enabling Pyongyang to earn the resources to move ahead with nuclear and missile programs. Kim Jong-un may be a little unlike his father and grandfather in some respects. However, undeniable is that he has no intention of North Korean denuclearization. The two Trump-Kim summits were basically about the same key issue of North Korean denuclearization. Therefore, the failure of the second summit meant that the first summit had failed. The two failed summits have also taught us that it is always hard to distinguish between a tough—or perhaps insecure—negotiator and an honest one.[5]

Even for the eight-month period of US–North Korea diplomacy budding, between the two summits in Singapore and Hanoi, Kim Jong-un was consistently adding to his weapons arsenal and nuclear infrastructure. According to a *New York Times* report:

> And in the time between Mr. Trump and Mr. Kim's first meeting, in Singapore in June, and their second in Hanoi, intelligence estimates suggest that North Korea produced enough uranium and plutonium to fuel a half-dozen new nuclear warheads. The evidence that North Korea was moving ahead with its weapons program was clear, according to American intelligence officials familiar with the briefings provided to Mr. Trump.[6]

Legitimate questions are raised regarding the two futile summits that had excited the whole world so much. Among others, why the Trump administration needed such summits in the first place and how many times more it needs to be fooled by the North Korean despot. Despite the huge effort American analysts and intelligence services have made to offer best analyses of the possibility of a denuclearized North Korea, most of them have proved to be half-truths at best. Their Achilles heel is the limited capacity to have their fingers on the pulse of the North Korean regime. For this reason, they are inclined to compare North Korea's military posture with that of a few Middle Eastern countries, notably Libya, Iran, and Iraq. These three countries in the Middle East offer no parallel to North

Korea in terms of a possible US war against a militant, dictatorial state. The United States has fought in all of the three countries. It fought one war with Iran in the late 1980s. America has engaged in the Iraq War since 2003 in one form or another, which led to the overthrow of Saddam Hussein's government, and his execution in 2006. As in Iran, NATO—of which the United States is the key player, with its financial contribution amounting to about 70 percent of the alliance's total spending—led military intervention in Libya to support rebels trying to overthrow Gaddafi's regime and ended his dictatorship in 2011, as noted above.

All of these US or US-led NATO wars were possible as they met a few primary prerequisites, notably minimizing civilian casualties thanks to geopolitical conditions more favorable for warfare than a second war on the Korean Peninsula, which will result in a huge number of civilian as well as military casualties as noted. Some analysts have argued that US troops stationed in South Korea are "nuclear hostages"[7] for North Korea. Therefore, it would sound reasonable to say that the Kim dynasty would be the first to oppose at heart a pullout of US ground troops from South Korea, although it is speaking to the contrary. Some 28,500 US troops stationed in South Korea have also been a great diplomatic capital for North Korea's deal with the United States,[8] as seen in the first Trump-Kim summit. In fact, Kim expressed willingness to give up the North Korean demand for US troops' removal from South Korea as a precondition for discussions over denuclearizing the Korean Peninsula.[9] A US military action against Pyongyang would also certainly invite strong reactions from China and Russia neighboring North Korea.

However, circumstances surrounding the Korean Peninsula may provide both North Korea and America with opportunities rather than risks. Kim Jong-un must already have realized that the geopolitical conditions of East Asia are very different from those of the Middle East, especially when it comes to international terrorism. Iran's support for terrorist organizations throughout the Middle East has been well known. The US invasion of Iraq that began in 2003 only disclosed that Saddam Hussein "did not have an active nuclear-weapons program, but that he was unable to come completely clean, in part because he had to keep his adversaries guessing."[10] The United States in particular remained greatly shocked in the wake of a series of four coordinated terrorist attacks by the Islamic terrorist group al-Qaeda against the United States on September 11, 2001. Saddam Hussein was suspected of having conspired with al-Qaeda to launch the terrorist attacks on the United States,[11] but the consensus of US intelligence experts was that there was no evidence of ties between Saddam Hussein and al-Qaeda.[12] Like Iraq, Libya is a haven and stronghold for international terrorists like Islamic State of Iraq and the Levant (ISIL) and al-Qaeda. Gaddafi in particular was condemned by many countries as he financed international terrorism. Most importantly, Kim Jong-un should realize that his perception of the linkage between Gaddafi's shameful death and his nuclear weapons program is utterly wrong. Gaddafi was killed by rebels because of his despotism and maladministration of national affairs, not because of the lack of nuclear weapons.

East Asia, unlike the Middle East, is not Islamic by religion, either. Nor does it provide shelters and fortresses to international terrorists. Although North Korea itself is currently on the list of state sponsors of terrorism, there has been no proven link between the Kim Jong-un regime and extremist Islamic terrorists who have harbors in the Middle East. Kim Jong-un, if he does not carry out terrorist acts himself—like the sinking of the South Korean warship *Cheonan*—and does not help international terrorists, cannot be subject to the kind of US anti-terrorism attacks that Saddam Hussein and Muammar Gaddafi had suffered. China and Russia, which are not Islamic states either, have joined campaigns against international terrorism, and have little reason to encourage a link between North Korea and Islamic extremists in the Middle East. Although Russia has maintained a strong and friendly relationship with the Syrian dictator Bashar Hafez al-Assad and assassinated dissidents at home and abroad, the country has yet to be qualified to be a state sponsor of terrorism as it is not considered a state that has "repeatedly provided support for acts of international terrorism," as the criteria for being on the list defined by the US state department says.[13] Russia has no known direct link with any of terrorist groups operating in the Middle East.

One of the major US purposes of dismantling North Korean nuclear and missile development programs reflects the long-standing US worry that North Korea's WMDs, notably nuclear materials, may be handed over to international terrorist groups, such as ISIL and al-Qaeda. The United States is still obsessed with the September 11 terror attacks and considers North Korea as a rogue state that could develop some sort of a cooperative connection with any terrorist group. Since Kim Jong-un is yet left clear of such a link, he has a lot of diplomatic capital to use in his negotiations with the United States for dismantling his nuclear program. Washington is not much concerned about the dictatorial character of the Kim Jong-un regime, as reflected in President Trump's remark that he "fell in love" with Kim. This policy stance of Trump meets at least two of the key objectives Kim wants to get from Washington in return for an abandonment of his nuclear program: a US guarantee of the Kim regime security—no interference in North Korea's internal matters—and a US–North Korea peace treaty that would accompany a diplomatic relationship between the two countries.

However, all this is conceivable theoretically only. The key question is still about whether Kim is really serious about denuclearization. No magic is available that can read Kim's true mind. Since the summit in Singapore, Kim Jong-un has taken some goodwill gestures toward the United States. According to a new analysis of satellite imagery released on July 23, 2018, by Airbus Defence and Space headquartered in Germany, North Korea had begun dismantling portions of missile test site at the Sohae station. On July 27, 2018, North Korea returned what was believed to be the remains of fifty-five American servicemen killed during the Korean War. On September 9, 2018, no nukes and ICBMs were on display during the military parade in Pyongyang's Kim II Sung Square to mark the seventieth anniversary of North Korea's founding. As for inter-Korean relations, North and South Korea withdrew troops and firearms from twenty-two frontline guard posts to reduce tensions between the two sides. In October, 2018, the rival two Koreas began removing mines and other explosives at two sites inside their heavily armed border as part of their tension-reduction steps. All the goodwill gestures and steps Kim Jung-un has taken can be considered as North Korea's confidence-building measures.

Yet, any analyst would like to look closely at any seemingly good move the world's last Stalinist country has taken. Kim Jong-un could implement at little cost all the seemingly confidence-building measures, such as the return of the remains of American soldiers and the decision not to display nukes and ICBMs during North Korea's celebrations. Goodwill gestures like these are reversible and have little to do with a North Korean denuclearization.

As for the partial dismantling of the Sohae missile test site, neither foreign experts nor journalists were allowed in to inspect the disassembling. Little is known about the Sohae site and much has been pieced together from analysts' assessments and the North Korean state-run media. Although 38 North, a prominent North Korea monitoring group, called the North Korean move "an important first step towards fulfilling a commitment," which North Korean leader Kim Jong-un made at his Singapore summit with US president Trump, Melissa Hanham, a senior research associate at the James Martin Center for Nonproliferation Studies in California, called it "the bare minimum that can be done at the site." "North Korea does not need the Sohae engine test stand anymore if it is confident in the engine design," she wrote on Twitter. As Kim said himself, North Korea is moving from testing to mass production.[14] "In satellite images, other important facilities like fuel bunkers, a main assembly building and the gantry tower remain untouched."[15] It remains unclear whether North Korea planned to raze the entire Sohae site, which has been central to its space program. Pyongyang has accused Washington of making a "unilateral, gangster-like demand for denuclearization" while offering the North little in return. North Korea officially says it no longer needs nuclear or missile tests because it has completed building nuclear-tipped ICBMs and begun mass-producing them."[16]

Despite all these plausible analyses, how has the Achilles heel of American analysts of North Korean affairs been unveiled specifically? Look back at the first Trump-Kim summit. Before the summit, the US president said that he "has been preparing for the encounter his entire adult life."[17] In fact, he made a bold decision to revive the talks that were once dead. Many analysts argued that the summit would be a nothing-to-lose match only for North Korean leader Kim Jong-un. They maintained, among others, that a sitting US president's talks with Kim Jong-un would serve to elevate Kim's stature on the world stage. This view derived from a plausible but blemished analysis. They failed to realize that if the summit flopped in substance at the end of the day, Kim's international status would further be damaged and even threatened, as such a miscarriage would only reveal Kim's determination to keep his nuclear program intact. If it really happened, the United States would have more reason to tighten its pressure on North Korea. The summit was a nothing-to-lose game for President Trump, too. In fact, the failure of the second summit in Hanoi demonstrated that Kim Jong-un has become a wretched loser on the world stage.

Needless to repeat, North Korea is one of the most dangerous states posing dire threats to the security of the United States, South Korea, and the rest of international society. The more dangerous a state is, the more efforts they should have made to draw it to the negotiating table, valuing mutual recognition and the spirit of compromise, especially given the reality in which a military strike, surgical or otherwise, against the North is almost unfeasible. On the contrary, they have made little effort to encourage a sitting US president to meet a North Korean leader. Pyongyang has been seeking a meeting with an incumbent American president for more than twenty years. Twenty years ago, North Korea was not eligible to be even a marginal nuclear weapon state.

American analysts and policy makers as well have lacked the ability to figure out effective diplomacy toward North Korea. Economic sanctions on North Korea are absolutely the most powerful weapon to stifle the NKNP and should continue until Pyongyang dumps nuclear weapons. With that said, naming and renaming it a state sponsor of terrorism in an inconsistent fashion, blaming its human rights violations, and threatening it with a possible military strike, such as "fire and fury," have been about all they could ever figure out on the diplomatic front concerning the NKNP. The diplomatic knack to effectively deal with North

Korea requires common sense. A common sense–based diplomacy to the NKNP should prefer talking to intransigence. Other than economic sanctions that need to be strengthened as much as possible, the United States has had only two options to resolve the NKNP: talks or a military attack.

If talking is the only realistic option, US diplomacy toward North Korea should have been much more aggressive in meeting with North Korean leaders, dead or alive, even in the form of the ruptured summit in Hanoi. Also, Washington should have been able to craft much more effective diplomatic narratives to use toward North Korea. The US government has surprisingly fallen short of this latter ability in particular. For example, shortly before the Singapore summit, US vice president Mike Pence and national security adviser John Bolton proposed the so-called Libya model for North Korean nuclear disarmament, which is, as indicated, the most horrible scenario that Kim Jong-un could accept, although Kim Jong-un must have a misconception of the relationship between Gaddafi's miserable downfall and his abandonment of nuclear weapons program. They should have tried to imagine what it would feel like to be in Kim Jong-un's situation. They also wanted to include North Korean human rights problems in the US agendas for the first summit. They should have not mentioned any words associated with a "Pyongyang Spring." They should have realized that in a democracy guaranteeing human rights matters but it would never come smoothly in any backward country without substantial socioeconomic development, which takes a long time.

For a summit—past or forthcoming—to succeed realistically, Trump needs to recognize that Kim Jong-un would remain a permanent leader of North Korea. The US president should continue to encourage Kim to become a North Korean Deng Xiaoping. Trump's assertion that "North Korea will become a great economic and financial nation one day" was realistic, as it made no reference to North Korean politics and showed US willingness to help Pyongyang prosper economically after a North Korean denuclearization.

A denuclearized Pyongyang would mean that the key basis of Kim regime's security would shift from militarism to economic development following economic reforms similar to those of China or Vietnam. Not only US formal guarantee of regime security and economic aid for North Korea but also time is required for this transition to happen smoothly. The United States and the rest of international society should help such a soft landing to occur in North Korea since it would serve the stability of not only North Korea but also the rest of the international community comprising East Asia.

The unrealistic "a grand bargain" that went well beyond the North Korean nuclear issue and was proposed to Pyongyang when the six-party talks started in 2003 to rescue North Korea's broken economy in return for its abandonment of nuclear weapons program[18] needs to be revisited in this context. Whatever else may be said of a post-denuclearized North Korea, the United States must pursue only one goal in its talks with North Korea, which is a permanent denuclearization (PD) of North Korea. Complete, verifiable, and irreversible dismantlement (CVID) is a redundant term that reflects unproductive skepticism and may unnecessarily irk Kim Jong-un. PD says it all. If only Kim Jong-un is found to be genuinely committed to PD, how to carry out it is secondary, be it a step-by-step or package resolution. Once the top-level US–North Korea talks have started, the two countries should make every possible effort to build up the momentum for the talks, although the Hanoi summit ended in failure. Needless to repeat, the United States should be wary of its past mistake to repeat encouraging North Korean leaders' bad habit of trying to extort resources from the international community in exchange for false cutback of its nuclear weapons program, not for PD. In this respect, Trump's decision not to reach an agreement with North Korea, which obviously tried to repeat the precedent of lying for economic benefits, was well advised. Kim Jong-un, on his part, should realize that the United States and the rest of the international community will never repeat their mistake of rewarding him for any of his offers for false denuclearization.

Whatever the possible actions for a North Korean denuclearization both Washington and Pyongyang could take for mutual benefits down the road, the key question is back to square one. Repeatedly, "Is Kim Jong-un really authentic in his commitment to working toward denuclearization?" Although it is not easy to answer this question, human sense often works better than the efforts for scientific verification and finds quite well how the wind blows, as indicated at the beginning of this book.

To recap, Kim Jong-un's dishonesty, if any, concerning his commitment to denuclearization will not last long, especially when the international community has been educated enough not to be conned by the North's regime any more. Qualified social scientists, be they theists or atheists individually, would never quote what the Bible says, to validate anything. Also, Kim Jong-un would surely reject any relationship between god and humans and rather believe in the personality cult surrounding the Kim dynasty. Nonetheless, when it comes to the relationship between one's honesty and fate, Kim may need to refer to the following quote from Proverbs 27-18 of the Bible: "Be honest and you will be safe. If you are dishonest, you will suddenly fall." This quote could even be considered a scientific assumption for empirical testing.

In the final analysis, President Trump, his associates and post-Trump US administrations could discover Kim's true intentions toward his nuclear program during their talks with Kim if they put the following into practice. They, President Trump in particular, should try their best to look at Kim's eyes rather than listen to his words during upcoming summits, if any. It would still be difficult for them to perfectly read Kim's mind, but Kim Jong-un, on his part, is believed to have known well by now that it is unfeasible to fool the United States any longer. The North Korean leader may also have been educated enough by this time to realize that the Kim dynasty's decades-long nuclear development program has only ruined the country and put his regime's survival at risk. If he puts into practice this realization, it will certainly ensure the security of his life and regime. Who knows? A Nobel Peace Prize may jointly be awarded to Kim and Trump.

The Highs and Lows of North Korean Nuclear Negotiations

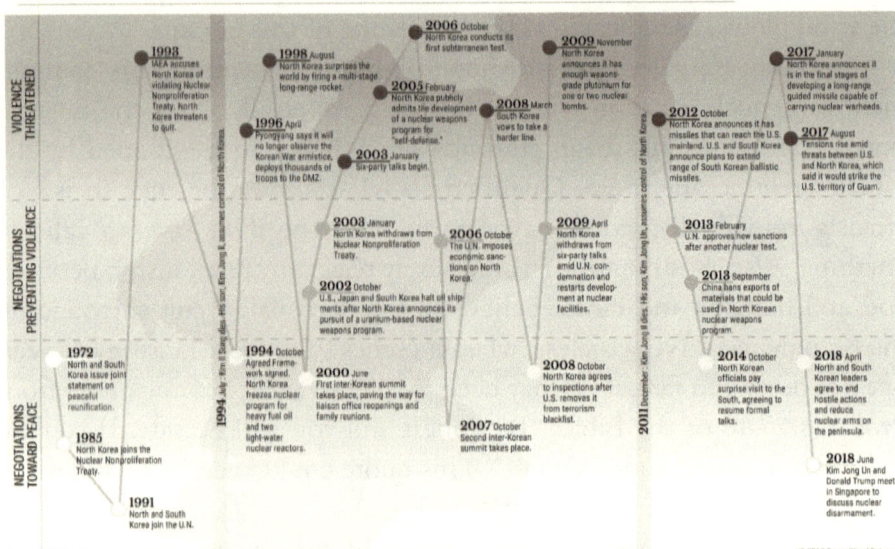

(Source: Geopolitical Futures 2018)
*See Appendix A for an enlarged image of this on, p. 190

Notes:

1 See, for example, J. Borger, "Trump-Kim Summit in Hanoi Collapses after Negotiations Fail," *Guardian* (2018), https://www.theguardian.com/, accessed February 28, 2019.

2 M. Boot, "A Summit without Substance," *Washington Post* (2018), https://www.washingtonpost.com/, accessed June 12, 2018.

3 Quoted in R. Gramer and E. Tamkin, "Decades of U.S. Diplomacy with North Korea: A Timeline."

4 E. Brewer and J. Pak, "How to Tell When North Korea Starts to Denuclearize."

5 Ibid.

6 D. Sanger and W. Broad, "New Images of North Korea Buildup Confront Trump's Hopes for Disarmament," *New York Times* (2019), https://www.nytimes.com/, accessed March 10, 2019.

7 T. Carpenter and D. Bandow, *The Korean Conundrum: America's Troubled Relations with North and South Korea* (New York: St. Martin's Press, 2004).

8 For reference to such concessions, see, for example, A. Ward, "North Korea Is Already Getting Concessions Ahead of Trump-Kim Talks," *Vox* (2018), https://www.vox.com/, accessed May 18, 2018.

9 E. McKirdy, "North Korea Drops Withdrawal of US Forces as Condition of Denuclearization, Moon Says," *CNN* (2018), https://edition.cnn.com/, accessed April 20, 2018.

10 E. Brewer and J. Pak, "How to Tell When North Korea Starts to Denuclearize," *Atlantic* (2018), https://www.theatlantic.com/, accessed October 10, 2018.

11 "President Bush Outlines Iraqi Threat," White House (2002), a White House press release (2002), accessed July 30, 2010. The press release said, "Iraq could decide on any given day to provide a biological or chemical weapon to a terrorist group or individual terrorists. Alliance with terrorists could allow the Iraqi regime to attack America without leaving any fingerprints."

12 J. Weisman, "Saddam Had No links to Al-Qaeda," *The Age* (2006), https://www.theage.com.au/, accessed October 30, 2017.

13 See, for example, D. Byman, "Russia Is a State Sponsor of Terrorism: But Don't Treat It that Way," Brookings Institution (2018), https://www.brookings.edu/, accessed April 30, 2018.

14 J. Johnson, "North Korea Begins Dismantling Key Missile Test Site, Satellite Imagery Suggests," *Japan Times* (2018), https://www.japantimes.co.jp/, accessed July 24, 2018.

15 S. Choe, "North Korea Starts Dismantling Key Missile Facilities, Report Says," *New York Times* (2018), https://www.nytimes.com/, accessed July 23, 2018.

16 Ibid.

17 M. Landler, "For Trump, Life's Been Preparation for Kim," *New York Times* (2018), https://www.nytimes.com/, accessed June 11, 2018.

18 See, for example, M. Hanlon and M. Mochizuki, "Economic Reform and Military Downsizing: A Key to Solving the North Korean Nuclear Crisis?" Brookings Institution (2003), https://www.brookings.edu/, accessed September 1, 2003.

CHAPTER 12

THE COMING FALL OF NORTH KOREA

To say the conclusion first, the North's Kim regime will collapse under the weight of its own nuclear weapons. If it had not been for the NKNP, the history of North Korea would have been written very differently. Kim Il-sung should not have learned how to build nuclear weapons but learned from Deng Xiaoping how to make North Korea prosper through economic reforms and compete constructively with South Korea and Japan, with no need to worry about international sanctions, let alone a possible US military strike. However, from the start, Kim Il-sung took a self-destructive course that would bring calamity on himself, his own people, his own state, his neighbors, and the peace-loving international community at large. The Korean War that Kim Il-sung provoked brought the first major risk to the life of Kim Il-sung himself. The war nearly killed Kim when a US intervention pushed his forces back to the Yalu River, according to Hong Kong–based writer M. O'Neill. He continues that:

> He [Kim Il-sung] had assured Stalin and Mao Zedong that he could conquer the whole peninsula before the US could intervene. He was responsible for the defeat. The second great risk came in 1956, after Nikita Khrushchev denounced Stalin in Moscow. That provoked an outpouring of criticism of Kim Il-sung, Stalin's protégé.[1]

Kim Il-sung survived the dangers that he brought upon himself and continued provocations against South Korea, the United States, and Japan, committing a variety of crimes against humanity. Kim Il-sung is the founder of the systematic and pervasive human rights abuses taking place today in North Korea. Kim Il-Sung's birthday is known as the "Day of the Sun" and is the most important national holiday of the year in North Korea, but Kim had turned the North into a land of complete darkness and threw hundreds of thousands into a hidden system of remote gulag work-camps from which few ever returned.[2]

As stated in Introduction of this book, "The Coming Fall of North Korea" does not mean the collapse of North Korea as a state. It means the breakdown of the Kim dynasty regime. North Korea as a state, called the DPRK, may still demise and be united into one Korea led by South Korea under the influence of the United States someday. However, the collapse of the Kim dynasty regime will not automatically lead to a Korean reunification. As we will see below, a North Korean regime change and a Korean reunification are two very different issues. The "one country, two systems" formula of China is also entirely irrelevant to two Koreas even in an impressionistic Korean confederation framework. The vast difference in political history—which includes the background of the emergence of the "one country, two systems" concept —of the Korean Peninsula and China explains this irrelevance in the first place.

For many years, analysts have predicted an impending downfall of the North Korean regime, trying to offer plausible scenarios. Since 1990s, US analysts have even tried to suggest what the United States and the rest of international society might do when the North Korean regime "finally succumbed to the inevitable consequence of its own insanity" as a self-induced famine ravaged the country,[3] as if it were a fait accompli. The most critical common flaw in their predictions has been the empirical basis to support them. History tells us few regimes have fallen due to national famine or even insanity in a short time—in several years. The despotic Kim dynasty has survived for seven decades. Most tyrannical regimes fell as a result of wars in which foreign powers were involved or in domestic situations that countenance popular uprisings supported by foreign forces. Saddam Hussein government fell after a coalition led by the United States invaded Iraq. Libyan dictator Gaddafi was killed in a civil war, in which NATO intervened militarily on the side of the anti-Gaddafi militants. A few totalitarian governments fell or were radically transformed as their leaders took new directions for the future of their nations. For example, the collapse of the Soviet Union started in the late 1980s and was complete in a few years as Soviet leader Gorbachev started to transform the political situation and the obsolete command economy.

The North Korean state or the DPRK will survive an end of the Kim Jong-un regime as Iraq and Libya survived the fall of the Saddam Hussein and the Muammar Gaddafi regime. Similarly, Russia survived the collapse of the Soviet Union that was a colonial empire as a collective of colonies that were bound to be ultimately independent. For now, an immediate North Korean regime change can happen through only one route—a coup in Pyongyang under the support of, if not masterminded outright by, China. North Korea is one of the 193 member states of the UN. Anyone who goes after political power wishes to be the head of a state, often at any price. Whatever the theories of politics, the core objective of real politics is to gain power. The politically ambitious like to take any actions necessary to achieve their ultimate objective of gaining supreme power. Anybody in the North who comes to power through a successful coup will refuse to go along with a unified Korea under South Korean law in which it is certain that they will lose power and even their lives or be put behind bars. China is most likely to support a coup when it determines the Kim dynasty of the North is against its national interest, after which the Korean Peninsula will still remain divided into two Koreas, however.

As indicated, despite all the rationalist notions that argue a reunified Korea under South Korea's democratic political system would be a win-win for nearly everyone[4] in East Asia—certainly except for the Kim dynasty regime—China still remains ambivalent about a reunified Korea. What China should do for its greater interest is one thing, and what China is actually doing is quite another. Like political leaders of many other authoritarian countries, Chinese leaders are caught up in outdated modes of thought. They have yet to better understand how they should manage their government and foreign relations for the improvement of their citizens' lives in this century.[5]

Given this Chinese shortcoming, the analysts who think that a reunified Korea will come with the downfall of the Kim Jong-un regime fail to see at least two major problems. The first is that the Kim regime would not fall without Chinese intervention. The second one is that China would neither support nor recognize a coup that would topple the Kim regime outside the framework of two Koreas on the Korean Peninsula. China is still the decisive player that can make a final verdict on the fate of the Kim Jong-un regime. It can squeeze North Korea's neck, and is likely to do so. Despite Pyongyang's considerable arsenal of nuclear weapons, missiles, and the "newly developed ultramodern tactical weapons" that Kim Jong-un bragged about recently,[6] the Kim regime is fundamentally vulnerable in every aspect of politics, economy, and society. "China provides Pyongyang with ninety percent of its energy imports and most of the food going to its military,"[7] which means the Kim regime cannot survive not only economically but also militarily without Chinese aid. China's negative signal, if conveyed clearly and strongly to the Kim regime, could be enough to lead to the regime's fall. China is likely to take the steps that will result in the demise of the Kim regime for the following reasons.

First, despite all the clamor about the brotherly friendship between China and North Korea, China's tolerance of North Korea's nuclear weapons is running out, as indicated. Even before North Korea's sixth test of a nuclear bomb on September 3, 2017, China had warned North Korea not to go past the "point of no return" with another nuclear test.[8] Beijing's North Korea policy has long been criticized for its irrationality as it increases anti-Chinese resentment across the world and support for America's military presence in Asia.[9] To recap, Beijing's support or benign neglect of Pyongyang's nuclear development will only work to China's strategic disadvantage. US security analyst Jamie Metzl writes:

North Korea's continued nuclear weapons push will justify the U.S. military's ongoing rebalancing to the Asia-Pacific, the acceleration of missile defenses in

South Korea and Japan that will undermine China's
nuclear deterrent, and Japan's active reconsideration
of its military capabilities.[10]

China must be redoing the cost-benefit analysis of North Korea as a
nuclear-armed state to help Beijing counter US military influence in East
Asia and Pyongyang's negative impact on China's multifaceted interest.
China will be reluctant to trade North Korea's role—conceivable at best
and most likely exaggerated—as its ally to pose a threat to US military
presence in East Asia—a presence that has done no harm to China's security in the region so far—with its long-time dependence on the US market
for its exports and its need to cooperate with Washington in all other
respects for its interest. Washington, which knows well that the backbone
of Xi Jinping's authoritarian presidency lies in China's constant economic
growth, is ready to continue the current trade war with China as an effective way to pressure the North Korean single ally to take aggressive steps
to stop the NKNP. In other words, the US trade war with China, even
if it is not expected to last long, is beyond trade and is targeted at North
Korea.

China already knows well that the United States is the last country
to attack it militarily unless it first provokes an unjustifiable war with
Washington or in East Asia in the first place. China remembers that even
back in 1951, when the Korean War was raging, the United States completely withdrew its initial plan to use nuclear weapons against the Chinese
intervention in the war. In 1950–1951, "America's nuclear monopoly
remained largely intact. The first Soviet bomb test had been conducted
in August 1949; the first Soviet air drop would not be made until late
September 1951. China was years away from its first test."[11] The prob-
ability of a major Sino-American war would be much smaller than that of
a very unlikely nuclear war between India and Pakistan that "could usher
in a nuclear winter and spell doom not only for South Asia but for a much
wider area surrounding the subcontinent."[12]

Second, Beijing is already aware that its support of North Korea
has worsened its international competitiveness. Apart from its support

of North Korea, global public opinion has long been censorious about China's violations of democratic rights, human rights, environmental sustainability, and international law.[13] It is a well-established fact by now that a nation's brand has a lot to do with its global competition.[14] All democratic citizens across the world know that China's alliance with North Korea is destabilizing global security. They know that China is not eligible to be and even should not be a global superpower as far as it remains an international hypocrite supporting the NKNP as North Korea's closest ally. To put it another way, they know that if China becomes a hegemonic global power, it would be a disaster to world peace. All told, China's support of Pyongyang has damaged its global interest since the international community of responsible states knows well that the world would be much better off without the NKNP. As early as 2013, analyst Ben Rhode had noted:

> When Beijing gave Pyongyang diplomatic cover after North Korean forces sank the South Korean corvette *Cheonan* and shelled Yeonpyeong Island in 2010, it damaged China's image and strengthened cooperation between South Korea, Japan and the United States.[15]

Third, North Korea is getting increasingly boisterous toward China as it is growing mature as a nuclear-armed state. North Korea even says that it "will never beg for the maintenance of friendship with China, risking its nuclear program which is as precious as its own life, no matter how valuable the friendship is."[16] North Korea claims that China is crossing a "red line" in its relationship with Pyongyang.[17] All in all, China has grown weary of its increasingly disobedient ally North Korea. North Korea's successive nuclear tests and missile tests have gradually rattled China. The Chinese consider the bad behavior of North Korea as a slur to China. "Obviously, it is an insult to China," said Cheng Xiaohe, an international politics professor at Beijing's Renmin University.[18] By a long shot, it is not China but North Korea that is crossing the red line. Various indications began to emerge in earnest from 2017 that China is losing patience with North Korea.[19] On top of that, the Kim Jong-un regime is already trying to play Beijing and Washington against each other, and come out the winner,[20] which neither China nor the United States will accept.

Fourth, North Korea has become an important domestic political challenge for the Chinese political leadership to address. Chinese leader Xi Jinping will never put up with North Korea at the cost of his broad-based popular support. Favorable views of North Korea among Chinese people have been receding. According to a 2014 *BBC World Service* Poll, 20 percent of Chinese people view North Korea's influence positively, with 46 percent expressing a negative view.[21] The "lips and teeth" relationship between China and North Korea has been deteriorating rapidly as Beijing thinks of Pyongyang as incapable of anything sensible today.[22]

Needless to say, besides China's pressure on the Kim Jong-un regime, many other factors are heralding the impending demise of the Kim dynasty of the North. To reemphasize, the global community has been so fed up with the world's longest-reigning autocratic family, the successive Kims of North Korea obsessed with nuclear weapons, that it wants to see the dangerous regime disappear from this planet. In 2011, a *Guardian* article introduced the ugly truth about North Korea's Kim dynasty:

> In her book *Nothing to Envy: Ordinary Lives in North Korea* (2009), the journalist Barbara Demick writes: "If you look at satellite photographs of the far east by night, you'll see a large splotch curiously lacking in light. This area of darkness is the Democratic People's Republic of Korea." The country has a chronic lack of fuel and food. North Korea, writes Demick, "is simply a blank." In truth, it has been effaced by one family.[23]

Emerging technologies may take actions to end the Kim dynasty rule even earlier than Chinese actions and the international pressure against the Kim regime. It is a no-brainer that technology has played a major role in changing the world. Technologies to be used to remove or capture global troublemakers, including national dictators, are making unremitting progress. Suffice it to say that physically invisible, undetectable, tiny drones loaded with the genetic information about any global mischief-maker could be deployed in any place where they work or reside to eliminate them. In 2015, a drone, too small and flying too low to be detected by radar, disturbed the White House.[24] Even more realistically, advances in technologies are improving the accuracy of the US THAAD system to an incredible extent. The "conventional" THAAD system is already being replaced by upgraded artificial intelligence–based missile defense systems that are perfectly accurate and thus make nuclear-armed missiles useless.[25] The upgrades to the US THAAD system in the Asia-Pacific are outpacing the North Korean missile development.[26]

Many will now begin to think of the possible steps that the Kim Jong-un regime may take for its own survival. In fact, the Kim Jong-un regime could still survive, depending upon what directions Kim is going to take. Kim Jong-un should realize that he came to the two US–North Korea summits held in Singapore and Vietnam as an intrinsic loser whose days are being counted, not as an intimidating national leader who could formally cap off and strengthen North Korea's international status as a nuclear-armed state as a result of any summit with a sitting US president. Whatever summit he had or will have and whoever he met or will meet in the future, most people in the world regard North Korea as an abnormal state that possesses nothing but nuclear weapons of no constructive or even military value. Generally speaking, nukes have actually become of no use anywhere in the world. Nuclear-armed North Korea can never be an example for any responsible country of the global community to follow.

Still, Kim has a chance to be a winner. International society has long recommended that North Korea pursue Vietnam-style economic growth "enough to take care of the basic survival needs of its people, get out of its extortionate habit of trying to use dangerous weapons programs to gain hard currency, and stop counterfeiting and drug running."[27] If the Kim Jong-un regime accepts this advice for active engagement with international society, it will be able to survive the internal and external conditions that have been endangering the regime's existence. Kim Jong-un will be welcomed with open arms into the global community of dynamic economies. To review, Vietnam is proof of how a broken economy can be revitalized through economic opening. The socialist-oriented market economy showcases successful economic reforms and industrialization. The *SCMP* reports on the remarkable success of the Vietnamese economy:

> Vietnam introduced sweeping market reforms known as *doi moi* from 1986 that saw its per capita GDP grow five times to US$2,400 today. The country now ranks among the fastest-growing economies in the world, with GDP growth of over 7 per cent in 2018.[28]

Washington, in particular, has advised Pyongyang for a long time to adopt the Vietnam model of economic progress. North Korea has showed willingness to follow the Vietnam model of a mixed economy. However, Kim Jong-un failed once again to convince the international community of his genuine willingness to abandon nuclear weapons in the Vietnam summit. Kim seems to have been impressed by the remarkable economic growth Vietnam has achieved but has already established himself as leader of a nuclear-armed state. Kim Jong-un seems to be trying to turn North Korea into a nuclear-armed Vietnam, but the United States will never accept his scheme and will keep tightening its sanctions against his regime. Kim needs to realize that the economic success of Vietnam, communist-run but with capitalist leanings, has been possible since it had no nuclear weapons development program and thus could be a friend to the United States.

It is admitted that even if the Kim Jong-un regime accepts the international advice to follow Vietnam-style economic reforms, it will take a considerable time for North Korea to repair its deep-seated economic troubles. Therefore, North Korea needs to start economic reforms and denuclearization simultaneously, as soon as possible. North Korea may eventually decide to go in this direction, but step by step for obvious reasons. This stage-by-stage approach will require economic aid and incentives from international society. However, until the international community can be fully convinced of Kim Jong-un's genuine intention for PD, it should faithfully comply with the established international criteria for PD. In this context, it cannot be emphasized enough that the partial denuclearization Kim had offered in the Hanoi summit is nothing but another "Big Lie." It is understandable that during the period of "compliance," the Kim regime may dismantle its nuclear program step by step but it should do that honestly and willingly, cooperating closely with international inspectors of its entire nuclear weapons program. An international reward for even "partial" dismantlement of North Korea's nuclear program at the first stage may be negotiable, if international inspectors are completely sure that Kim Jong-un is honestly committed to PD. In fact, a one-shot nuclear dismantlement in a short time—like in a few months—may be realistically impossible but the Kim Jong-un regime should honestly divulge its nuclear weapons development activities in their entirety in Yongbyon, Kangson, and all other hidden sites to begin with, and should be able to convince international inspectors that a "partial" or a "first-stage" dismantlement is enough to disable any possible attempt by Pyongyang to resume its nuclear activities.

As for the "authentic intention" for PD, North Korean leader Kim Jong-un must realize again that humankind is living in an era that does not require nuclear weapons for any reason and any purpose. Some commentators suggested that Kim Jong-un has received plastic surgery to make himself look so like his grandfather Kim Il-sung.[29] It is not important whether this allegation is true or not. Kim Jong-un doesn't need to try to be like his grandfather in terms of threatening world peace and security. The world's two longest-ruling nonroyal national leaders, Fidel Castro of Cuba and Kim's grandfather Kim Il-sung, could maintain absolute despotism for about half a century without or almost without nuclear weapons. Kim Il-sung, in particular, died of a sudden heart attack, not of a lack of nuclear weapons. At the time of his death in 1994, North Korea's nuclear weapons were just fledgling. Kim Il-sung might have foolishly thought nuclear weapons could ensure his permanent rule over and security of North Korea, and even his permanent life span. Indeed, Kim Il-sung was declared in 1998 "Eternal President" of North Korea, which, however, all reasonable people on this planet are scoffing at. In whichever way we may see our time, the twenty-first century is different from the days of Kim Il-sung's rule over the North.

The Korean War or "the Kim Il-sung War" needs to be reviewed here from a twenty-first-century perspective. Such is the case since the war needs to be seen with emphasis on megatrends of this century. Megatrends of our era feature weakening human stupidity and growing human wisdom, defying Albert Einstein's famous remark that human stupidity is infinite. Human stupidity as reflected in the Korean War simply does not fit the inexorable directions this century is taking. More specifically, such trends already started around the time when the North-South Korea hot war ended on July 27, 1953, with an armistice signed. Steven Pinker, Pulitzer prize-winning professor of psychology at Harvard University, observes that we are currently heading toward a more peaceful world. "Today we may be living in the most peaceful era in our species' existence," he says. Pinker continues that we are enjoying the longest period of some seventy years of the most peaceful world after World War II.[30] His observation indicates that WMDs have no value at all in the current global structure featuring close interconnectedness.

Without nuclear weapons and with a mixed economic system that blends market economy with socialism, like that of China or Vietnam, Kim Jong-un can still ensure his permanent position as supreme leader of his country. Kim may need to relax a little the absolute control he exerts over his people in order for him to emulate Vietnam. But such relaxation will not endanger his position as supreme leader of North Korea. In fact, unlike the dynastic North, one-party Vietnam has not been ruled by a single strongman ruler since the late 1980s, and tolerates some personal freedom,[31] but it has been able to maintain total control of people's political rights.[32] Kim also needs to look at Xi Jinping's permanent presidency and his iron grip over the Chinese people. Chinese nukes have nothing to do with Xi's permanent presidency. Kim can be a North Korean Xi Jinping if he succeeds in Chinese or Vietnam style economic reforms for North Korea. Considering his days are already numbered, he will have nothing to lose if he follows the Chinese or Vietnam model of economic success.

Unfortunately, North Korean leader Kim Jong-un put to shame the fanfare for the second US–North Korea summit in Vietnam. It may also be too early to conclude that a third US–North Korea summit will never happen. At any rate, hard facts support the view that he must be continuing nuclear work. Reportedly, a North Korean senior general was executed in 2018 shortly after the first summit in Singapore as he told his colleagues that they no longer needed to suffer to make nuclear weapons.[33] US secretary of state Mike Pompeo said on June 27, 2018, that North Korea still poses a nuclear threat, disputing US president Trump's earlier claim that "there is no longer a nuclear threat from North Korea."[34] On the same day when Pompeo made the statement, US mainstream media reported that satellite images showed North Korea was upgrading nuclear facility at its Yongbyon Nuclear Scientific Research Center, validating the criticism that Trump's meeting with Kim in Singapore had produced no verifiable proof that North Korea will discontinue its nuclear program.[35] Trump conceded on July 1, 2018, that a deal with North Korea may not work out.[36]

No new dismantlement activity at the engine test stand of North Korea's Yongbyon nuclear research site from August 3 to September 27, 2018. A satellite image captured on August 3, 2018 (Source: Airbus Defence & Space and 38 North/Pleiades © CNES 2019, Distribution Airbus DS)
*See Appendix B for an enlarged image of this on, p. 191

Before the Hanoi summit, US president Trump seemed rather optimistic about a North Korean denuclearization in his State of the Union address on February 6, 2019. Trump said, "Much work remains to be done, but my relationship with Kim Jong-un is a good one." Especially after the failed Hanoi summit, the belief that Kim Jong-un's nuclear ambition will never be dead still remains prevalent in the educated world. Kim Jong-un has already proved himself to be a deceitful talker, not a genuine doer as his offer in Vietnam of partial denuclearization demonstrates. When Kim Jong-un managed to have Donald Trump revive the first summit that Trump had once canceled, critics contended the summit would only validate the long-lasting bad behavior of the Kim dynasty regime. Such criticism already seemed valid shortly after the Singapore summit since North Korea failed to show no significant actions for denuclearization. Analysts said to the effect that "in the end, what this summit achieved was have the US president indirectly legitimize a notorious dictator."[37] In an opinion article published right after the summit, the *Washington Post* summarized the results of the summit:

> The Singapore summit was, without question, a triumph for Kim Jong Un. A dictator who has ordered the murder of his own family members, and who oversees a gulag comparable to those of Hitler and Stalin, was able to parade on the global stage as a legitimate statesman, praised by the president of the United States as "very talented" and worthy of trust. President Trump offered Mr. Kim a major concession, the suspension of U.S. military exercises with South Korea. Mr. Kim, meanwhile, did not commit to the "complete, verifiable and irreversible" denuclearization the United States has demanded.[38]

US intelligence services reportedly suspect that North Korea has now nuclear weapons and facilities at multiple secret sites. US intelligence services' suspicion about North Korea's ongoing nuclear activities is based on hard evidence.[39] It is therefore no wonder that analysts believe that Kim deceived US president Trump and ended up as the winner from the first summit in Singapore.

However, this notion is subject to a critical review. It would be silly of you to believe you would never fall to serious injury or death when you climb a tall tree. Kim Jong-un could reach the crown of a tall tree thanks to the first summit but he seems now at a loss, not knowing how to come down safely. Kim could have believed he had succeeded in glorifying his coronation as tsar of a nuclear-armed state on the world stage by meeting a US president in Singapore. Moreover, Kim seems to have had every confidence that he can deceive the United States into loosening sanctions against North Korea, get economic aid, end US–South Korea joint military drills, and so on. If Kim Jong-un had been allowed to take the partial denuclearization step in the Vietnam summit in return for a lifting or loosening of US sanctions against him, he would have believed he could make his country a nuclear-armed Vietnam. When he tried to cheat Trump in Hanoi for the second time, the US president chose to end the summit abruptly. Kim seems now at a loss, not knowing how to come down safely from the "tall tree" he climbed up in the first summit.

For this reason, the two Donald Trump–Kim Jong-un encounters in Singapore and Hanoi still matter, regardless of the lack of the talks' substance or failure. The Kim dynasty of the North has provided the United States with enough chances to recollect the quip from C. JoyBell C., an American thinker and writer: "Don't let a thief into your house three times. The first time was enough. The second time was a chance. The third time means you're stupid." Washington is not stupid and won't provide Pyongyang with anything substantial unless it is sure of Kim Jong-un's genuine determination to surrender his nuclear program. The red carpet that Kim Jong-un walked on in Singapore and Vietnam could turn into death row for him if the United States becomes perfectly sure that Kim came to the two summits as a wolf in sheep's clothing.

Kim should be aware in particular that Donald Trump is a business mogul–turned president. Trump knows how to do business. The US leader will never make stupid investments, such as lifting US economic sanctions on North Korea, unless he is perfectly sure of a North Korean denuclearization. If Kim ever thinks he could cheat Trump, believing Trump's rhetorical remarks about him, such as "very honorable," "very talented," or "fell in love," the North Korean leader is dealing with a wrong person. Such diplomatic expressions are commonly used in the business world.

The North Korean tyrant might have enjoyed a mental placebo to make him feel better or euphoric after signing the vague document in Singapore. However, it would never have made his problems go away. Rather, his problem had only deepened since he obviously repeated the North's bad behavior of cheating the international community in Vietnam. The failed Hanoi summit has worsened Kim Jong-un regime's notoriety and isolated North Korea further from the rest of the world.

Kim Jong-un has already crossed the Rubicon. If he behaves himself toward international society, he will survive; otherwise he and his regime will come to a tragic end. The North's regime has lived on the ropes for too long to hang in there any longer. To conclude, the only option Kim Jong-un can take for his own survival is to follow the nuclear-free and prosperous Vietnam model of economic success.

Notes:

1 M. O'Neill, "Kim Il-sung's Secret History."
2 See, for example, "North Korea: Kim Il-Sung's Catastrophic Rights Legacy: End Ongoing Discrimination, Abductions and Enforced Disappearances," Human Rights Watch (2016), https://www.hrw.org/, accessed April 13, 2016.
3 J. Metzl, "Why North Korea Is Destined to Collapse."
4 Ibid.
5 For a similar line of argument, see J. Soto, "The Weakening of Representative Democracy," *Outlook on the Global Agenda 2015*, World Economic Forum (2015), available at: https://www.weforum.org/, accessed February 26, 2015.

6 See, for example, H. Kim and M. Lee, "North Korea Deports American, Boasts of 'Ultramodern' Weapon," *PBS* (2018), https://www.pbs.org/, accessed November 16, 2018.

7 J. Metzl, "Why North Korea Is Destined to Collapse."

8 See, for example, L. Dearden, "China Warns North Korea Another Nuclear Weapons Test Would Take Relations beyond 'Point of No Return'," *Independent* (2018), https://www.independent.co.uk/, accessed April 25, 2017.

9 See, for example, B. Rhode, "China, North Korea and the Spread of Nuclear Weapons," Belfer Center for Science and International Affairs of Harvard Kennedy School (2013), https://www.belfercenter.org/, accessed June 30, 2013.

10 J. Metzl, "Why North Korea Is Destined to Collapse."

11 C. Posey, "How the Korean War Almost Went Nuclear," *Air & Space Magazine* (2015), https://www.airspacemag.com/, accessed May 17, 2017.

12 M. Ayoob, "India and Pakistan: Inching toward Their Final War?" *National Interest* (2018), https://nationalinterest.org/, accessed March 14, 2018.

13 See, for example, A. Corr, "Why North Korea Cannot Have Nuclear Weapons, but Japan and South Korea Should," *Forbes* (2017), https://www.forbes.com/, accessed April 30, 2017.

14 See, for example, P. Kerr and G. Wiseman, *Diplomacy in a Globalizing World: Theories and Practice* (New York: Oxford University Press, 2013), 354.

15 B. Rhode, "China, North Korea and the Spread of Nuclear Weapons."

16 B. Lendon, C. Luu, and S. Han, "North Korea: China Stomping on 'Red Line' in Relations," *CNN* (2017), https://edition.cnn.com/, accessed May 4, 2017.

17 Ibid.

18 J. M. Frayer, "China Grows Weary of Its Unruly Neighbor North Korea," *NBC News* (2017), https://www.nbcnews.com/news/, accessed September 7, 2017.

19 T. Yu, "China's Leaders, People Losing Patience with North Korea," UPI (2017), https://www.upi.com/, accessed April 11, 2017.

20 A. Fifield, "North Korea Tries to Play Beijing and Washington against Each Other—and Come out the Winner," *Washington Post* (2018), https://www.washingtonpost.com/, accessed September 10, 2018.

21 "2014 World Service Poll," *BBC* (2014), https://www.bbc.com/, accessed December 30, 2014.

22 K. Brown, "What Does China Really Think of North Korea?—Forget Talk of 'Lips and Teeth'—Chinese Contempt for North Korea Is Palpable," *Diplomat* (2018), https://thediplomat.com/, accessed May 25, 2018.

23 I. Sansom, "Great Dynasties of the World: The Kims of North Korea," *Guardian* (2011), https://www.theguardian.com/, accessed April 30, 2011.

24 D. Schneider, "Can We Detect Small Drones Like the One That Crashed at White House? Yes, We Can," *IEEE Spectrum* (2015), https://spectrum.ieee.org/, accessed February 3, 2015.

25 See, for example, A. Behrens "Joint Air and Missile Defense Mission Command: A Singular, Intelligent Multi-Domain Platform and Culture," An unclassified paper submitted to the Faculty of the United States Naval War College, Newport, Rhode Island (May 29, 2018), 33.

26 See, for example, M. Chan and J. Lee, "US Targets Chinese and Russian Missiles with THAAD Upgrade in South Korea: Military Analysts," *South China Morning Post* (2018), https://www.scmp.com/, accessed July 17, 2018.

27 M. Hanlon and M. Mochizuki, "Economic Reform and Military Downsizing: A Key to Solving the North Korean Nuclear Crisis?"

28 J. Power, "The Second Trump-Kim Summit Will Boost North Korea. Could It Gain Even More from Vietnam?" *South China Morning Post* (2019), https://www.scmp.com/, accessed February 12, 2019.

29 M. O'Neill, "Kim Il-sung's Secret History."

30 J. Weston, "The Moral Arc Reconsidered: Empirical Evidence that the Arc of the Moral Universe Bends toward Justice," *UU World* (2013), http://archive.uuworld.org/, accessed April 20, 2013.

31 M. Pennington, "Trump Says He's 'in No Rush' after N. Korea Talks Postponed," *Stars and Stripes* (2018), https://www.stripes.com/, accessed November 7, 2018.

32 According to *Freedom in the World 2019* report of the Freedom House, both China and Vietnam are among "Not Free" countries in political rights and civil liberties. The authoritarian governments of the two countries partially allow civil liberties of their citizens, but completely oppress their political rights. Freedom House (2019), https://freedomhouse.org/, accessed February 27, 2019.

33 J. Ryall, "North Korea 'Executes Officer Who Jumped Gun on Peace on Peninsula'," *Telegraph* (2018), https://www.telegraph.co.uk/, accessed June 28, 2018.

34 See, for example, D. Sanger and W. Broad, "Once 'No Longer a Nuclear Threat,' North Korea Now in Standoff with U.S.," *New York Times* (2018), https://www.nytimes.com/, accessed August 10, 2018.

35 See, for example, J. Cheng, "North Korea Is Rapidly Upgrading Nuclear Site Despite Summit Vow," *Wall Street Journal* (2018), https://www.wsj.com/, accessed June 27, 2018.

36 See, for example, T. McCarthy and M. Pengelly, "Trump: 'Possible' North Korea Nuclear Deal May Not 'Work Out'," *Guardian* (2018), https://www.theguardian.com/, accessed July 1, 2018.

37 See, for example, R. J. Heydarian, "Kim Jong-un Came Out Victorious from the Summit," *Al Jazeera* (2018), https://www.aljazeera.com/, accessed June 13, 2018.

38 Editorial Board, "No More Concessions," *Washington Post* (2018), https://www.washingtonpost.com/, accessed June 12, 2018.

39 See, for example, N. Smith, "North Korea Expands Weapons Facilities Despite US Pressure to Disarm," *Telegraph* (2018), https://www.telegraph.co.uk/, accessed July 2, 2018.

EPILOGUE

A strong wind began to blow at a greater velocity and the waters grew rough. Wind waves were growing larger when a cargo ship took off far from a port. It was loaded with overweight goods at the port. Due to unbalanced weight of the goods, which included deadly weapons, the ship began to lean and was about to capsize in the growing waves at any minute. The sea captain was utterly at a loss what to do. He transmitted distress calls and received a response that said, "Sink all the goods on board into the water." He did so, and he and his ship barely survived the looming disaster. His insurance company even compensated for the cargo he dumped into the water. If he had not done so, he would have lost his life and everything else.

Kim Jong-un regime's ship is loaded with nuclear weapons, long-range missiles, and other WMDs. It remains to be seen if Kim Jong-un will be smart enough to give up nuclear weapons to keep alive none other than himself and his regime, and to bring prosperity to his country, which remains completely ruined primarily due to Kim dynasty's paranoid love affair with nuclear weapons.

Kim Jong-un said on April 15, 2012, in his first speech in public since assuming the leadership of North Korea, "The days are gone forever when our enemies could blackmail us with nuclear bombs."[1] He was dead wrong. Kim should have said instead, "The days have come when our nuclear bombs could be self-destructive to us."

Despite the fact that the uselessness of nuclear weapons was proved already during the Korean War, the Kim dynasty of North Korea has threatened the peace and security of the international community with nuclear weapons. The contradiction is that the educated world knows well the worthlessness of nuclear weapons but it has been scared by North Korea's nuclear weapons development. Fortunately, the educated world has been becoming more educated and has now come close to the conclusion that Kim Jong-un's nuclear business, even if it is unstoppable by any means, may be none of our business, and we cannot but let the Kim regime keep doing what it wants to do at the cost of its life. Yes, there is a possibility that a cash-strapped or vengeful North Korea could sell one of its warheads to a terrorist group for the right price.[2] However, all powerful countries in the world, including North Korea's single lifeline China, have been jointly staging a war against terrorism. The day North Korea is found to be ready to sell a single nuclear warhead to a terrorist group would mean the end of the Kim Jong-un regime. Advances in science and technology have already entered a stage where they can detect in advance what the Kim regime is going to do. Kim, who is "very talented," knows enough of this. US president Trump was right when he said the United States was "in no rush" for nuclear talks with North Korea.

As long as North Korea remains nuclearized, US economic sanctions against it will become more intense. US national security adviser John Bolton warned just one week after an "agreement" between Trump and Kim Jong-un fell apart in Vietnam that "more sanctions against North Korea may be coming."[3] Simultaneously, US economic relations with China are most likely to deteriorate further, hurting the Chinese economy and putting the popular support for the Xi Jinping government at risk. China is the second largest economy in the world, but its per capita nominal gross domestic product (GDP) stood at 8,643 US dollars in 2018, only 14.5 percent of that of the United States in the same year.[4] Confronted with economic problems with the United States, China cannot but see the Kim Jong-un regime dying according to its own choice. It is correct to say North Korea is now left with only nukes that have no military value within the contemporary global structure, a bankrupt economy, and despotism.

Luckily for the Kim Jong-un regime that is becoming extinct, a road leading to a Washington-Pyongyang big deal still remains open for the survival of the Kim Jong-un regime. A big deal for a North Korean denuclearization would surely include US security guarantee for the Kim Jong-un regime as well as a large-scale economic assistance to North Korea. It is admitted that for a US–North Korea nuclear deal to happen realistically, Washington too should concede what it should concede in a bona fide quid pro quo agreement. However, US authentic willingness to make such concessions—which is already obvious—is secondary. Whenever Kim Jong-un is going to meet a US president, any other US official, or a foreign leader for nuclear talks, he should ask himself if he has genuine willingness to abandon his nuclear weapons. If the answer is no, he should be aware that his regime will collapse soon. Going a step further, he needs to ask himself two fundamental questions. The first is "Have nukes made North Korea strong?" The second, "Are nukes realistically useful to North Korea even for military purposes, under the current world structure?"

A sweeping popular uprising of starving North Koreans is also invisibly simmering, another significant factor that can lead to a downfall of the Kim dynasty. In fact, continuing generational change in North Korea has already become a potentially serious political challenge that the Kim dynasty regime has to address. The bulk of the North Korean population, especially the younger population struggling with starvation and an unpromising future, is finding no difference between death from hunger and getting killed during a popular rebellion.

As Kim Jong-un has hit a snag with his obvious intention to gain concessions from the United States without denuclearization, the young dictator of North Korea met with Russian president Vladimir Putin on April 25, 2019. The summit between the two authoritarian rulers seemed to send a signal to Washington that Kim was expanding his diplomatic chess game.[5] Underneath Kim's smiles during his first-ever talks with Putin was also a stark message to US president Donald Trump that the United States is not the only game in town.[6] In fact, the Russian leader has been saying that North Korea's nuclear issue should be discussed in the six-party framework, in an apparent effort to indicate that Russia is not merely an onlooker in the US-North Korea nuclear deal. However, the Putin-Kim meeting as well as Kim's message to Trump will hardly have any significant impact on the US position toward Kim's nuclear weapons.

I cannot reemphasize enough the following point that I highlighted already. It is admitted that Kim Jong-un's decision to open up North Korea to the outside world requires huge courage and candor to let the world as well as his own people know the dark records of the North's history, which include the fabrication of the Mount Paektu Bloodline,[7] the personality cult for the Kim dynasty, Kim Il-sung's decision to invade the South, the existence of the gulag work-camps equal to those of Hitler and Stalin, and the murderous acts that Kim Jong-un himself committed against his family members and subordinates. On the face of it, it seems hardly possible for Kim Jong-un to make any of those outrageous lies and misconducts better known to the whole world, especially to his own country. It seems plausible to argue that communist countries, such as China, Vietnam, Cuba, and Laos, were able to open up to the international community, as they have no such a stumbling block to opening as North Korea's Mount Paektu Bloodline, the backbone of the legitimacy of the Kim dynasty.[8]

However, a closer look at such notions reveals that they are not quite well-advised. All communist countries, including those that have opened up to the outside world, have their own dirty history,[9] which is equivalent to North Korea's. For most North Koreans, starving and undernourished, the truth or untruth of the Mount Paektu Bloodline must matter little. What matters most to them is the bread-and-butter issue. Everything else, even political oppression, is secondary to them. As indicated, Kim Jong-un's fear that North Korean nuclear scientists, for example, would let the world know what the Kim dynasty of the North has been doing, once freed in the wake of opening, especially in connection with North Korea's secret development of nuclear weapons and other WMDs, is quite understandable. However, Kim needs to be more afraid that without successful reforms of the North Korean economy, the chances for his regime's survival will continue to shrink until its ultimate termination, certainly in a few years.

North Koreans have steadily defected from their country to South Korea, China, Russia and other countries across the world for economic, ideological, religious, political and other reasons. They already know quite well the bogus Mount Paektu Bloodline, reject the personality cult surrounding the ruling Kim family, and scoff at the NKNP or the *Songun* policy that has caused the expanded poverty in North Korea. In South

Korea alone, there were 31,339 North Korean defectors as of 2017, compared to 947 in 1998.[10] To put it another way, North Korean defectors and even family members of the Kim dynasty ousted from power have disclosed to the world all the fakeries of the Mount Paektu Bloodline and the personality cult for the three-generation Kim family.[11] It would be no exaggeration to say that the world is left with little to know more about the falsehoods of the Kim lineage that North Koreans have been forced to worship.

Given this reality, Kim Jong-un's bold confession of past misdeeds to start a new, prosperous era for his nation must be well-advised and will certainly serve him and his regime best. Such a self-assured move will be able to make him an audacious hero—indeed, deserving even a Nobel Peace Prize. To recap, this will be the only way for Kim, who is already on the ropes, to survive. Not only the international community but also North Koreans will forgive the past misdeeds of Kim's grandfather, father, and Kim Jong-un himself, if Kim Jong-un takes audacious initiatives for economic reforms for his country to feed his countrymen.

This move by Kim Jong-un to fundamentally recast North Korea would mean the foundation of the Kim regime's legitimacy shifts from the self-destructive Mount Paektu Bloodline, which will not last long anyway, to a constructive, internationally acclaimed economic prosperity, which will ensure Kim Jong-un's lasting rule over North Korea. To reemphasize, Kim Jong-un should learn more from China's success. An overwhelming majority of the Chinese will not protest against the communist one-party dictatorship as long as the Chinese economy is doing fine and feeding them well. As this keeps happening, Chinese leader Xi Jinping will be able to continue to enjoy high popularity among his people. As for the "Big Lie" of the Mount Paektu Bloodline, Kim Jong-un should also realize that China, too, has been called an "Empire of Lies,"[12] which may put to shame even the "Big Lie" of North Korea. It would be simply absurd for Kim Jong-un to try to hold on to the suicidal Mount Paektu Bloodline, for the maintenance of which he tries to keep fostering tensions with the international community through nuclear brinkmanship, especially with the North Korean economy continuing to contract. Such a silly move by Kim, valuing nukes and other WMDs, if sustained, will end his regime soon.

In sum, if the Kim Jong-un regime dismisses the last option remaining for its continued existence at this time, it will demise, most likely in five years, due to its own nukes that it wrongly believes will protect its life and bring success to North Korea. Looking back, it was the best time for North Korea to launch Vietnam-style economic and social reforms when the young Kim Jong-un assumed office as supreme leader of North Korea in 2011. At that time, Kim Jong-un should have introduced thorough reform policies for the North Korean economy, winning wide-ranging international support in return for abandoning his nuclear arsenal. If he had done so, he could have established himself as a heroic leader of a country that deserves international admiration. Kim seems to have lost the best opportunity to do so, but, luckily for him, it is still never too late to reform the reclusive country. The Kim Jong-un regime is now at the crossroads between prosperity and collapse.

On June 30, 2019, Donald Trump had a surprise encounter with Kim Jong-un at the DMZ. With the highly symbolic gesture, Trump became the first sitting US president to set foot on North Korean soil. Would the historic, dramatic event be any significant for the future of the Kim Jong-un regime? It remains to be seen.

Notes:
1 S. Choe, "North Korean Leader Stresses Need for Strong Military," *New York Times* (2012), https://www.nytimes.com/, accessed April 15, 2012.
2 See, for instance, J. Borger and I. Sample, "All You Wanted to Know about Nuclear War but Were too Afraid to Ask," *Guardian* (2018), https://www.theguardian.com/, accessed July 16, 2018.

3 See, for instance, J. Tacopino, "John Bolton Warns North Korea Could Face Even More Sanctions," *New York Post* (2019), https://nypost.com/, accessed March 6, 2019.

4 *World Economic Outlook Database*, International Monetary Fund (2018), https://www.imf.org/, accessed October 30, 2018.

5 S. Hiltner and K. Syckle, "Morning Briefing," *New York Times* (2019), https://www.nytimes.com/, accessed April 25, 2019.

6 See, for instance, A. Smith, "What's Really behind Kim Jong Un's Meeting with Putin?" *NBC News* (2019), https://www.nbcnews.com/, accessed April 25, 2019.

7 Ji Sue Lee, a South Korean analyst of North Korean affairs, argues that a North Korean opening would deal a fatal blow to the legitimacy of the Kim Jong-un regime based on the Mount Paektu Bloodline. See, J. Lee, "What Is Expected – An Inevitable Sudden Change in North Korea," a commentary (written in Korean) contributed to Korea America Friendship Society (2018), http://kafs.or.kr/, accessed April 16, 2019.

8 J. Lee, "What Is Expected – An Inevitable Sudden Change in North Korea."

9 See, for instance, I. Somin, "Lessons from a Century of Communism," *Washington Post* (2017), https://www.washingtonpost.com/, accessed November 7, 2017.

10 "Current Situation – Policy for North Korean Defectors (written in Korean)," Ministry of Unification of the Republic of Korea (2019), https://www.unikorea.go.kr/, accessed April 16, 2019.

11 See, for instance, M. Chang, "North Korea's Fabled Mount Paektu Bloodline," *Straight Times* (2017), https://www.straitstimes.com/, accessed February 28, 2017.

12 See, for example, G. Sorman, "The Empire of Lies: The Twenty-First Century Will Not Belong to China," *City Journal* (Spring 2007), https://www.city-journal.org/, accessed March 17, 2019.

INDEX

The Highs and Lows of North Korean Nuclear Negotiations

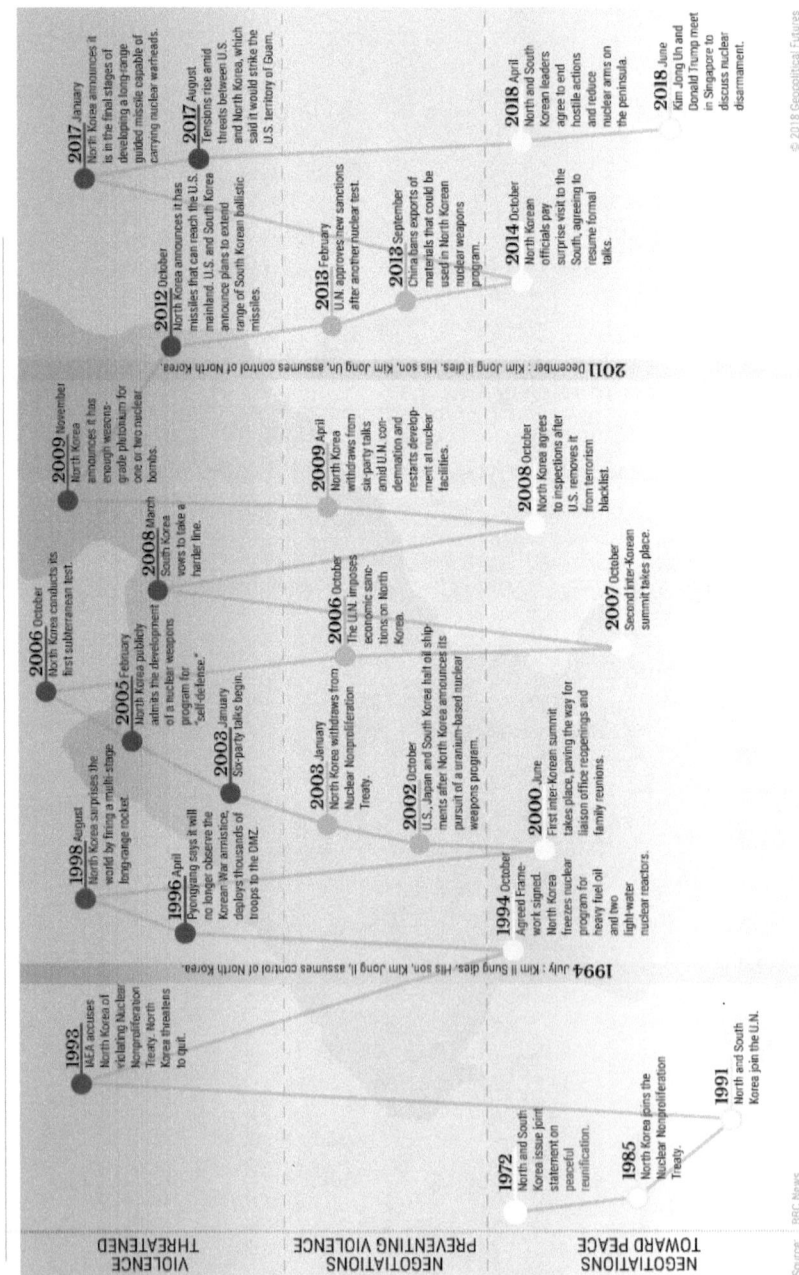

VIOLENCE THREATENED

1993 IAEA accuses North Korea of violating Nuclear Nonproliferation Treaty. North Korea threatens to quit.

1998 August North Korea surprises the world by firing a multi-stage long-range rocket.

2006 October North Korea conducts its first subterranean test.

2009 November North Korea announces it has enough weapons-grade plutonium for one or two nuclear bombs.

2017 January North Korea announces it is in the final stages of developing a long-range guided missile capable of carrying nuclear warheads.

2017 August Tensions rise amid threats between U.S. and North Korea, which said it would strike the U.S. territory of Guam.

NEGOTIATIONS PREVENTING VIOLENCE

1996 April Pyongyang says it will no longer observe the Korean War armistice, deploys thousands of troops to the DMZ.

2005 February North Korea publicly admits the development of a nuclear weapons program for "self-defense."

2003 January Six-party talks begin.

2003 January North Korea withdraws from Nuclear Nonproliferation Treaty.

2002 October U.S., Japan and South Korea halt oil shipments after North Korea announces its pursuit of a uranium-based nuclear weapons program.

2006 October The U.N. imposes economic sanctions on North Korea.

2008 March South Korea vows to take a harder line.

2009 April North Korea withdraws from six-party talks amid U.N. condemnation and restarts development at nuclear facilities.

2012 October North Korea announces it has missiles that can reach the U.S. mainland. U.S. and South Korea announce plans to extend range of South Korean ballistic missiles.

2013 February U.N. approves new sanctions after another nuclear test.

2013 September China bans exports of materials that could be used in North Korean nuclear weapons program.

NEGOTIATIONS TOWARD PEACE

1972 North and South Korea issue joint statement on peaceful reunification.

1985 North Korea joins the Nuclear Nonproliferation Treaty.

1991 North and South Korea join the U.N.

1994 October Agreed Framework signed. North Korea freezes nuclear program for heavy fuel oil and two light-water nuclear reactors.

2000 June First inter-Korean summit takes place, paving the way for liaison office reopenings and family reunions.

2007 October Second inter-Korean summit takes place.

2008 October North Korea agrees to inspections after U.S. removes it from terrorism blacklist.

2014 October North Korean officials pay surprise visit to the South, agreeing to resume formal talks.

2018 April North and South Korean leaders agree to end hostile actions and reduce nuclear arms on the peninsula.

2018 June Kim Jong Un and Donald Trump meet in Singapore to discuss nuclear disarmament.

1994 July : Kim Il Sung dies. His son, Kim Jong Il, assumes control of North Korea.

2011 December : Kim Jong Il dies. His son, Kim Jong Un, assumes control of North Korea.

Source : BBC News

© 2018 Geopolitical Futures

APPENDIX B

Airbus Defence & Space / 38 North
August 3, 2018

Pleiades © CNES 2018, Distribution Airbus DS

Old fuel/oxidizer bunkers
remain partially demolished

Test stand
components stacked

Approximately 7 vehicles/
trailers with cylindrical tanks

Old fuel/oxidizer bunkers
remain partially demolished

Some additional
dismantling of test
stand has occurred

New vegetation
growing in blast area

www.ingramcontent.com/pod-product-compliance
Lightning Source LLC
Chambersburg PA
CBHW022250290526
45785CB00015B/500